Patterns
of Grace

Patterns of Grace

Human Experience as Word of God

TOM F. DRIVER

FIRST EDITION

Designed by Jim Mennick

Library of Congress Cataloging in Publication Data

Driver, Tom Faw, 1925–
   PATTERNS OF GRACE.

   1. Christianity—Psychology. 2. Experience.
3. Word of God (Theology) 4. Creation.
5. Story-telling (Christian theology) 6. Gestalt
therapy. I. Title.
BR110.D74   201.'.9   77-14520
ISBN 0-06-062089-7

To four who taught me four ways of love:

ANNE BARSTOW

LEE HANCOCK

BEVERLY HARRISON

CAROLYN HEILBRUN

Contents

Writing is certainly born of secrecy, but we should not forget that either it tries to hide this secret and to lie—in which case it is without interest—or to give a glimpse of this secret, even to try to expose it. . . .

—JEAN-PAUL SARTRE

Preface

MY professional life has taken place entirely at Union
Theological Seminary in New York, where I began to teach
in 1956. Even earlier, in 1950–53, I was a student here and
came under the influence of Paul Tillich, one of the profound
minds and great teachers in the twentieth century. I am full
of both gratitude and irony when I consider that today I hold
the Paul J. Tillich Professorship of Theology and Culture,
having been given this honor soon after my own theology
began clearly to diverge from that of my mentor.

One day I was sitting with students on the floor of the
classroom. (In that course we always sit on the floor, if we
do not lie, stand, jump or dance on it.) One student began to
tell of his fierce hatred for a certain Texas landlord to whom
he had once paid rent and from whom he had taken much
abuse. All this was in the past except the hatred, which
festered on. The student was asking for help in clearing the
hatred away. Several of us worked on the matter for some
time, using techniques of Gestalt therapy that are indige-
nous to this theology course. When we had done as much as

we could, I paused, looked at the student and said, "Tell me about your theology." He turned to me in surprise. He had thought we were doing psychology. Then he said: "Sure. I believe that God is a great landlord in the sky. He has got it in for us, and there is nothing we can do. The only thing is to wait and hope that a savior will come along to intervene." He paused. Then the confession: "I know that's bad theology, and I've never written it in any of my papers, but it's what I think." The circle sat stunned. I said, "Please write it for this course." He did, and more besides. Both his anger and his theology began to flow. It is often not easy to admit what we truly think.

The ideas in this book have taken shape in my head as I have taught the course in which we sit on the floor. My main thought in the course is that our experiences have authority, as much in theology and faith as in any other part of our lives. It is a simple idea, yet I was moved to put it at the heart of a theology course because I noticed that students tended to divorce their academic work from their other experiences as if the latter, though somehow vaguely pertinent, had no authority. In myself I found a similar rift, in spite of my love of literature, which is founded on the authority of experience.

In that class on the floor, I sometimes deliver myself of ideas, theological assertions. The hardest question my students ask me, and they ask it every time, is, "Yes, we hear what you say, but how did you come to think it?" Tell me a story. I flinch, then try. To answer well, I would need to be an artist. To *see* one's experiences, to see how they fit together (or how they fall apart), and to communicate the sight—that is a creative task. One way God brings us to second birth, I believe, is to summon us to make a *life* out of countless experiences.

I want to thank my students for helping bring this book to birth. Without them, I would not have had courage to speak nor have known what to say. Much of what is here I learned from them. If they read it, I hope it will remind them of our adventures together in Room 205. There we literally wrestled, played angel and Jacob till I, at least, was wounded and blessed.

Those graduate students who tutored for me, giving me their trust as I experimented wildly with method, deserve to be mentioned by name: Christopher Morse, Dan Cawthon, Kevin Gordon, Ann Martin, Mike Mooney, George Kuykendall, and Jean Lambert. And Jean Lanier, too, who came as a "visiting scholar," stayed to co-teach, and put me, like all the rest, under discipline.

No statement I have made to my students seems to have meant more to them than the one I uttered one day after taking a long breath: "All my experience is Word of God for me." I hope my readers may be brought to some such awareness of their own experience and thus to feel with their senses the glory that is God. There is no tongue and no word, no joy, pain, good nor evil that does not resound with the presence of God. At least, that is how I figure it.

Look you and see.

Tom F. Driver

Union Theological Seminary
New York, 1977

Acknowledgements

To the faculty of the University of Otago, Dunedin, New Zealand, and particularly to Gavin D. Munro, Dean of Knox Theological Hall, for inviting me as William Evans Visiting Professor in 1976 and giving me the opportunity to present some of the material herein as a series of lectures.

To the organizers of the Conference on Theology and Body at Emory University, Atlanta, for inviting me in 1973, to give the personal reminiscence which is recounted in Chapter 1. In somewhat different form, this chapter was included in the book resulting from the conference: *Theology and Body*, ed. John Y. Fenton (Philadelphia: The Westminster Press, 1974).

To Sara Nicoll for typing my manuscript.

To Jacquelyn Grant, Barbara Wheeler, and Jerry White for reading and criticizing my first draft. And to Marie Cantlon, my editor at Harper & Row, who helped me to improve the second draft.

To Grove Press for permission to quote from "The Incarnate One" by Edwin Muir; and to Random House, Inc., for extracts from "What Shall I Chartreuse?" by Charles

Conroy, "The Sea and the Mirror" by W. H. Auden, and "The Snow Man" by Wallace Stevens.

All Biblical quotations, unless otherwise noted, are from the Revised Standard Version.

Introduction

My subject is rich, my arrangement of it musical. I can handle the subject only by the interplay of themes. I introduce these now by name. In subsequent chapters I combine and develop them. The concluding chapter is a coda wherein the themes are recapitulated and transposed. The book is logical, but the logic is not linear. It is musical.

The major theme is expressed in English by the word *pattern* and in German by *Gestalt*. I bring in the German word because it has already been used in several disciplines that are relevant to my meaning: psychology, theology, philosophy, and esthetics. Almost everyone has heard of Gestalt therapy, and it was in that context that the term first became important to me. I soon learned of its wider, richer connotations. For instance, in German, *Gestalt* is one of the words for a human face. Today, *Gestalt* has almost become a word in the English language. What does it mean, and why do we need it alongside our own word *pattern*?

A gestalt may be defined as "a structured, unified

whole."[1] That means a pattern, a design, a something we can recognize or identify. To speak of a gestalt reminds us, as the word *pattern* may not, that the objects and designs we recognize in life would not be recognized if we did not actively structure and unify the overwhelming sensations that flood upon us from our environment.

The patterns we make when we look upon our world are our experiences. We experience what we see, feel, hear, taste, smell. Knowing this obvious fact, we often forget that it is *we* who see, feel, hear, smell, and taste. We suppose that we merely register what's before us. We do take in, but we also give out in the very same act. Our taking in and our giving out result in an encounter of energies. The encounter of these energies precipitates form, which may be called pattern, gestalt, or "thing." Here comes the second theme.

I call the second theme *co-creation*. This is the one that puts me into conflict with most Christian theology. I don't believe that anything real comes from one, and only one, creator. For a long time now (starting way back in some parts of the Bible), Christian theology has been saying that creation is the work of God alone. This is what I, as a Christian theologian, am supposed to say, too. I'm going to say something else. I'm going to say that nothing comes from one alone. It takes *two* to tango. In the words of Martin Buber, "In the beginning is the relation."

I use a cluster of terms to express the theme of co-creation: *encounter, relation, interaction, intercourse,* and *transaction.* I am concerned with the theme epistemologically

[1] Frederick Perls, Paul Goodman, and Ralph Hefferline, *Gestalt Therapy* (New York: Delta Books, 1965), pp. 227f.

(how we know what we know), ethically (how we do and should assume responsibility), and theologically (how we are related to God). The theme is basically connected to certain thoughts about perception that I have taken from Gestalt psychology. Briefly, I mean that all our perceptions are patterns formed in our encounters with our milieu. We are born into a surrounding environment. Working together with it, we co-create our world. Part of the construction is communal and cultural. Part is individual. All is collaborative, the fruit of many kinds of intercourse between internal and external energies. John Donne said, "No man is an island. . . . Each is a part of the main." Whether we think of ourselves as islands of individuality or as parts of large continents of humanity (both images are appropriate), our creativity and our experiences take place at the shore. As Perls, Goodman, and Hefferline put it, "experience occurs at the boundary between the organism and its environment."[2] The interactions at this boundary produce our perceptions, generate the ethical issues we face, and bring us into contact with God.

In this book I shall not enter upon a systematic treatment of Gestalt psychology, the reasons I think Christian theology should prefer it to the depth psychologies of Freud and Jung, nor the the bearing of all this on ethics and Christology. Those are matters I hope to take up in a subsequent volume. Here I am composing a larger pattern, the better to suggest the holy and fateful character of our co-creativity with God.

[2] *Gestalt Therapy,* p. 227.

A third theme, then, is that of life's *change, flow,* and *flux.* As I am at odds with the thought that God creates alone, so am I also in disagreement with the idea that God does not change. I remember well when I first began to think of this, though it has taken me long to face the consequences.

I grew up in the border-South, where the difference between what changed and what did not was very important. We lived in the foothills of the Appalachian Mountains. They are very old, and the rate of change in their rock formations has become very slow. Most people who live there take the rocks for granted as the permanent, mostly hidden substructure. They delight in the growth of foliage above the rock and in the thought of the rock's permanence below. There are no earthquakes. The whole cosmos, including human nature and society, is seen on the model of permanence and change. Change is interesting and good if it does not affect the substructure. Affections are proper and nourishing so long as they do not move the foundations of character and morality. One should meditate upon eternal truths in order that the motion of life, pleasant in itself, not touch the fundaments.

I was thirty-seven years old before I crossed the American continent. That was in 1962. Earlier, I had traveled mostly northward and eastward. My longest journeys had been to Europe, the cultural rock in which the roots of American life, as I understood it, were set down.

In the spring of 1962, I flew to California to give some lectures at the Pacific School of Religion in Berkeley. From the air I got my first look at the barren reaches of Utah and Nevada. Without the green foliage I was used to, where was the life? I gave my lectures and came home to New York, a city built upon rock.

In the summer of the same year, I flew to California again and gave lectures at Lake Tahoe. There, my friend Dan Newman met me with his jeep, and we went bumping to the arid southwest which he, a painter and the son of a New York rabbi, had already come to love. We drove down to Yosemite, then over mountain passes to Tonapah, south to Navaho country, to Canyon de Cheilly, to Monument Valley, camping every night, and finally to Santa Fe. Sitting in the jeep hour after hour while the land passed by, I was amazed at the articulation of the rock. At Canyon de Cheilly, I saw how the rock had been laid down by the sea in sand, holding even now the patterns of the swirl of the water. At Monument Valley, I saw how the rock had been first heaved upward from the bowels of the earth, then carved away by wind, sand, and water. At the rim of the Grand Canyon, I saw how the Colorado River had cut like a knife into rising layers of rock, to reveal at every level breathtaking changes in color and texture of the flesh of earth. For the first time in my life, I heard the sense of the phrase, "the living rock."

I heard also the pulse in Ariel's lines:

Nothing of him that doth fade
But doth suffer a sea-change
Into something rich and strange.
—*The Tempest,* I, ii, 400–402

When I returned from that jeep ride, I set off again for Europe, this time to places new to me. I came to the valley of the Dordogne in France, which I found both fertile and dry. In caves above the river, Stone Age people had used rock formations to provide outlines and contours for paintings of powerful beasts. I came also to Greece, there to find the history of man, woman, and rock intertwined.

Since 1962, I have ceased to measure change by permanence. I came then to the thought I hold today: "All things change—some faster than others." And who holds the clock that measures fast and slow? You do, and I do. It is the rhythm of the beat of our hearts.

About ten years went by before I dared apply this thought to God. God, I now think, changes too. Sometimes I think God changes slower than I, and sometimes I think God changes more fast.

If we imagine change without form (which is nearly impossible to do), we come upon sheer flux, energy, and chaos. Chaos is not our experience, but the threat of chaos is part of every experience, for each experience is a gestalt that is shaped in the midst of chaos. According to Genesis 1, this situation is the same for God, who confronted (still confronts?) an "earth without form."

Announce now a fourth theme. This theme must enter as much without preparation as it does in Genesis 1. It has to do with the movement from chaos to form, from nothing to something, yet in such a way that chaos and mystery remain part of the very patterns which give form to the formless. I will call this theme *action*. It will have also to do with initiative, motive, and the authoring of one's experiences. This motif is very existential and, I think, equally biblical. I have set it out in dramatic fashion in the story I tell in the chapter called "God, Self, and Authority." The initiation of any act, therefore the quality of the act as a whole, cannot be accounted for nor explained. It cannot ever be described except by way of a dramatic narrative. Other forms invariably reduce (or eliminate) its mystery and vibrance, without which the phenomenon of an action is lost.

No doubt I touch here upon the reason why Jesus' principal utterances are aphorisms and parables. I am one of a number of theologians today who believe that theology has, in the course of time, removed itself too far from its roots in narrative. I find myself not only agreeing that theology originates in stories (and should itself tell more of them), but also thinking that all knowledge comes from a mode of understanding that is dramatic. Far from merely illustrating truths we already know some other way, the dramatic imagination is the means whereby we get started in any knowledge whatever. This suggests that the basic philosophical category or principle is action. I must therefore depart from Paul Tillich and many other philosophers and theologians who have held that the basic principle is Being.

Finally, there is in this book a motif I call *awareness*. It is closely realted to what is expressed often in theology as acceptance (Tillich), or "justification by faith" (Luther), and it is here influenced by Taoism as mediated through Gestalt therapy. I am on my way toward an ethic which begins and ends in an attitude of life acceptance, passing through moral choices in between. That is, in fact, the pattern of this book. The principal motif of the first chapter is awareness and acceptance of one's own body, which is the instrument of our thoughts and emotions. Whenever our awareness is heightened by unjudging acceptance of whatever is going on, we enter upon holy ground and are moved to praise. That is how my first chapter ends and what my final chapter is about. In between, I move through many twists, mazes, and contradictions. The pattern of the book is a simple model of the basic dramatic character of life: initial contact and awareness, then complications and frustrations as we are challenged to grow, and finally a renewed and enriched experience of unity.

To be sure, the third act or moment of that rather Hegelian dramatic pattern does not always occur. I am very mindful of lives cut off in frustration, of sufferings borne by millions in apparent futility, of crucifixions, holocausts, and systematic oppressions. I do mean, however, to say that the horror of these agonies is due to their contradiction of the pattern I have outlined. No adult person expects not to suffer. Equally, no adult expects that suffering should not lead one day to greater wisdom and holiness. When we despair of this, when we are worn out by suffering, we head into chaos—as did Macbeth when he exclaimed that life's "but a tale told by an idiot . . . signifying nothing" (V, v, ll. 27–28).

Here then are my five themes, intertwined, transposed, and played in several keys throughout the book:

Pattern
Co-creation
Change
Action
Awareness

Some may wonder (not after reading the book, I hope) what these have to do with Grace and the Word of God. I give a short answer right here.

The Word of God, as it is called, is not a word from the dictionary. It is not even that whole set of words collected in the Bible. It is not even those supplemented by the proclamations of preachers. God knows it is not the words I have written here. Rather, the Word of God is the patterns of experience (whatever they be) that move us to praise and enjoy our co-creator. For a Christian, the Word of God is, above all, the figure (pattern, gestalt) of Jesus. But this figure is dead when we do not collaborate with God to re-create it ever and again in our reading of Scripture and our encounters with other human beings. For this reason, traditionally called the work of the Spirit, the figure of Jesus changes. That means, the Word of God changes. If it did not change—if the Word of God were not free to adapt and re-pattern itself—it could not call us to action. Instead, it would lull us into sleep by constant repetition. In that case, the Word of God would be as dull as the church is much of the time. Instead of that, let us see that the Word of God is as fresh and lively, as full of change, as is the best of art and the most challenging of historical moments. Only if we allow the Word of God to change, I think, can we find our way to that holy ground where all is awareness, acceptance, praise, and the dance of heaven.

Tub Water and Holy Ground

THE theologian soaked in the bathtub.

It had been a late night: old friends talking of religion and psychology way into the morning. As so often in summer, the dawn light woke him, though his limbs were still tired. He got up and looked at the fog hanging at the tops of trees. It blocked out the sky and the mountains, a giant filter holding back most of the light of the sun.

Inside himself he felt foggy, too, yet restless with some old energy. The house was still, its three other occupants asleep, and the cat and the two Labradors. The house was large, a summer bungalow built in 1900 for a big family, some servants, and no telling how many guests. While it was not pretentious, its space and simple furnishing gave him a sense of luxury, as if the purpose of life were living, as if family life were a good thing provided there was space enough and time for each person to have some privacy. He turned his attention inward.

Tired limbs and untoned muscle spoke to him. "Wash us," they said. There was a chorus of complaint in his body. "Take care of me. Treat me with love."

He remembered that in forty-eight years and in spite of a deeply sensual nature he had never quite made peace with his body. It was one of several reasons why the knowledge had mocked him when he learned, long after growing up, that he was born under the sign of Gemini. Now his body, which at times was that "heavy bear" Delmore Schwartz made a poem about, was crying. If he did not respond, it might despair, grow sick, or (much worse) launch into a monologue as long and accusatory as the speech of Caliban in Auden's *The Sea and the Mirror*. He longed—or was it his body that longed?—for the sea. "Wash me. Take care of me."

The house had five bathrooms, and his was at the end of the hall. His bathing would disturb no one. The bathroom in his own summer house had no tub, only a shower stall. True, there was a swimming pool into which he would plunge once, maybe twice, a day. Yet there he tended to be rather aggressive, as in so much of his life, as if the purpose of living were to hurry. No doubt about it, and sensual as he might fancy himself to be, he had the disease of the Puritan Ethic, aggravated by technology and the media. Whatever he did, he wanted to do and be done with, the better to do something else. He would dive in the pool, get out, dive again. After several immersions he would splash a bit, churning the water. Then he would swim a few laps, get out, dry himself, done with it. He professed to enjoy this, and you could hear him exclaim how marvelous it was; but he noticed that in the middle of his dip his mind had already gone on to the next thing, even if he did not yet know what that would be. He lived eschatologically, always for the end, although he had long since ceased being able to imagine an end of history or time, or even the end of his own days. Therefore he lived for little, finite ends over and over, losing interest in episodes before their finish. He was good at starting and stopping—no, to be truthful, at starting and quitting, though he could often manage to end a speech or a letter with quite a flourish—but he was not good in the middle of the course. He had a problem with centering.

"Wash us."

He went into the bathroom and filled the tub with warm water. Then he sat down in it and began to wash himself. The idea was to wash every part, to bathe and caress every section of his skin, as if his were the body of a baby or a sick person to whom he might minister with rag, soap, water, and gentle touch.

"Wash me, and I shall be whiter than snow. Purge me and I shall be clean." It was not a prayer to God but an instruction to himself. Still, there was something incantatory about it, and he perceived that he was conducting some sort of ritual. Better, however, not to think too much about the known rituals of washing. His mind skipped lightly over the images of baptism, foot-washing, annointments with oil. The latter was especially strong for him because of a time in the dry heat of central Turkey when he had been invited to rest at a farmer's house and they had refreshed him by offering scented oil and showing him how to rub it on his face, hands, and feet—the first time he had ever felt the meaning of the word *balm*.

These images now were too liturgical, too biblical, and

therfore too dangerous to his present activity. They might interpret it for him before it had happened, which he sensed was the error of theology—always knowing too much—and which reinforced his own hurried tendency to skip over the middle of an act. So his mind turned for a languid moment to Leopold Bloom in the bathtub, and he re-Joyced once more in the Irishman's comically gorgeous image of his penis floating in the water like a lilly. Consider the lilies of the water. They toil not. Neither do they stiffen. Well, he had the gospel in his soul, and not even Joyce, who probably had it in his soul, too, would erase it.

Where he seemed not to have the gospel was in his body. He felt that if his body's longing for salvation could not be answered then he did not have the gospel at all. He knew enough to know that the gospel was not an idea but a deliverance. It was therefore an act. No act, not even an act of the mind, was conceivable bodiless. The gospel would bring good news to his body, or it would liberate nothing. Why had he never been told this? Once he thought of it, he knew it with absolute certainty: the fate of the self is the fate of the body, and the gospel is body-gospel; but none of his teachers had ever said so.

These thoughts rose in him and mercifully subsided. He returned to his limbs in the water. They were still waiting to be washed.

He started with his face, which he gave himself time to feel. Lightly he followed all the crevices in each ear. When he was in a hurry, all these irregular shapes and turnings in the ear bothered him. They could not be washed efficiently. But when the ear is explored at leisure, as he had already discovered in times of extended foreplay with his wife, it takes on a mysterious beauty. Was there a correlation between this and the mystery of oral communication? We do not look at the ears of a person to whom we talk, hardly so even when we whisper directly into them. The message goes into this incredible crevice, this cavernous antenna, and we look for the response elsewhere, in eyes, face, and movements of the whole body. In its combination of creviced ugliness and beauty, the ear is like a vagina and its lips. He wondered, for a second, if he had any right to explore his own ear so carefully, to get inside it with the probe of his finger. The more gentle his touch, the more he felt that he might offend some intimate and ultimate silence. But the ear gave itself to his feel, and the barrier was crossed into warmth and reverie.

He proceeded to his neck, arms, and shoulders. Here the contours were broad, his instinct to love uninhibited, the same reaction to his own body that he had to others'. He went on to his chest and stomach and all the way down his body. He washed his abdomen, his groin, and his genitals with mild erotic pleasure. He was not ashamed of these parts, not even of his anus, which he had learned in recent years to hold less tightly than before, having been, he feared, a rather tight-assed youth. He washed now his legs and his feet, and ended with the spaces between his toes.

To all this care his body responded. He could feel life stirring within him. His penis tingled, grew spongy, but not erect. It was in that state so pleasurable to men, midway between flacidity and frustration—a reminder of vitality without an imperative to action. It is a state of bemusement, not quite serious, not quite comic, which communicates well-being. He lay back in the water and smiled. He was happy.

After a moment it came to him that the ceremony was not finished. He could not think why, but he was sure it was true. If he followed his usual way, he would put aside such a slight feeling of incompletion. Life is never complete. Don't dally. The bath is over. Get out, dry yourself, go on. But he waited.

What was it that wanted to be done? The voices that had said, "Wash us," were still. Or almost so. It seemed as if one member of that chorus still made a murmuring sound. Not a word, not an entreaty, just a faint sound. Almost like a whimper of despair, yet hardly even that. Something wanted attention, but he did not know what, how, or why. He waited.

He lay back in the water and raised his knees. Then he reached out with his hand, touched his right knee, and moved his palm along his thigh. Then both hands, to encircle the thigh and stroke it all over. He did the same with the left one and realized he had come in contact now with a point of contradiction. No, the bath was not finished. More than that, something between his knees and his hips had never been finished, never seemed quite right or completed for as long as he could remember.

The very word *thigh* offended him. He had been conscious of this some time earlier and had even mentioned it to his wife, who thought he was crazy. When she spoke of chicken thighs, he winced. The proper term, which he had learned as a child, was *upper joint*. The word *thigh* reminded him of flesh too soft and skin too white. His unthought habit of mind seemed to deny that he had thighs at all. Legs, yes; but not thighs. If he went to the doctor about a rash, he might say, "It's on my thigh," but that was a purely objective statement. Indeed, he was more likely to point and say, "It's here." Something about a thigh he didn't like.

Now he continued to touch it. What was it he refused? Too soft and too white. Too much useless flesh. The flesh around his middle didn't bother him. True, his silhouette with the expanding waist was not attractive, but the stomach flesh itself felt good, and he liked to gather it in his hand. But not the flesh of his thigh. The sun never got to it, especially on the inner side. The fatty flesh of his two thighs sometimes rubbed together when he walked, which could not have been what God intended. He had no theological belief that flesh was sinful, but this flesh was. It harbored an alienation. At this place he was alienated from himself. The offending flesh was to be hid also from God.

What God had to do with his thighs, or they with God, he couldn't imagine. He searched his memory. The only thing he came up with was the line in Genesis about the angel touching Jacob on the thigh. He didn't know if that was important. He remembered some commentaries saying the expression was euphemistic, that it meant the angel had touched Jacob's testicles, because many ancient people swore by their balls. He could hardly think of a more powerful oath, but he didn't quite think in his own case that he had displaced a shame about his genitals to his thighs. Maybe he had, and ten years of analysis would prove it, but he was not now going to go on a bookish hypothesis with no internal hunch to support such a thought. More likely he had followed a child's logic after hearing the Genesis story and had hid his thighs from God so the angel wouldn't get to them and change his name and his life and make him a villain-hero like Jacob.

This thought came a little closer home. He did believe in election or religious destiny or whatever you call it. If there was something at odds between his thighs (or any part of himself) and God, it surely had to do with whatever he was supposed to become in the divine dispensation. But even this, while partly to the point, did not ring with full conviction. It was still too deductive, too literary an interpretation of feelings playing shy at the doorway of his mind.

The only thing of which he was sure was that his thighs were experienced in alienation. He had them in his thought as a burden of sin. This was the craziest idea that had ever occured to him. That is, it was crazy to take such an idea seriously. But obviously it was serious or he would never have dragged the thighs of chickens into it. Nor would he have been blocked in astonishment when his wife would say, in bed, that the most delicious part of the body was the soft inner flesh of the thigh. For a sensualist to draw a blank at such a statement, for him to be so perplexed that he couldn't even disagree and could merely mutter a yes, yes without believing it, was seriously crazy. Of course, he had an easy out. Everybody has hang-ups, and it's foolish to dwell on them. His wife had long since taken this attitude. While she knew he was crazy in this regard it didn't bother her because she thought everybody had the right to be crazy, except when he went out of his mind with anger at something, which it had never occurred to either of them to connect with his thighs, since you could see that his anger was in his flushed face, tight neck, threatening arms and fists. He was soon to discover more about this anger, but right now he was making some first, tentative connections with unknown territory.

The alienation in or from his upper legs had gone on so long that in the normal course of things the most he could be aware of it was the vague sensation of an inner despair, if it made any sense to think of a despair in one's leg. He carried sin in his flesh. He carried his sin in the rejected flesh of his thighs, which flesh, unused, unattended, unloved, had ever more lost its tone. It was—he tried to avoid the thought—carrion.

He wondered if he believed in Original Sin. This was, for the modern mind, the most offensive of all Christian doctrines, and certainly he was offended by it. He tended to agree with the French philosopher, Paul Ricoeur, that Original Sin is a pseudodoctrine, a piece of myth dressed up as a rational thought. Original Sin meant that you were born wrong, so that you couldn't do anything really right. And this condition was inherited, one generation from another, all the way from Adam and Eve. He had no truck with Augustine's version, which was that the sin is transmitted through the lust of the sex act in which we are conceived. Nor did he believe in the doctrine for the good Christian reason that it postulated the disease for which Christ was the cure. You ought not to invent a complaint in order to justify the remedy.

The doctrine of Original Sin stood in the way of one's

affirming the goodness of self, neighbor, and nature. To be sure, Original Sin warned you not to be surprised when people do evil, and this forewarning could lead to a certain charity of mind, as the theologian had learned long ago from Reinhold Niebuhr. But the problem didn't lie at this moral level. It lay deeper, at a level his teacher Paul Tillich would call ontological, and which he himself called the level of faith and celebration.

Any doctrine which clouded or inhibited one's joy to be alive was itself sinful, for it precluded spontaneous praise. Orthodox Christianity, dwelling on Original Sin, had become crabid. It could praise God for what He did an aeon ago on the first day of creation, for what He did in the so-called gift of His so-called begotten Son, and for what He would do at the end of time. It might even praise Him for certain managerial feats in the meantime, as in the idea of His providential control of history. But orthodox Christianity knew nothing of how to praise God (or anything else) for the sheer joy of it. Calvin, no less, had been astute enough to say that "the chief end of man is to glorify God and enjoy Him forever"; but Calvinism was joyless. Instead of taking pleasure, it seemed only to hope that the time will come when it might do so with a clear conscience. This was the dour fruit of the doctrine of Original Sin, and the theologian for that reason rejected it.

Whatever sin meant, it did not mean that the goodness of God and creation are at some necessary remove from us until the end of time. Nor that our only foretaste of it is mediated through the Christ. The whole problem with Christianity lay in this tendency to think that goodness is mediated. On the contrary, he thought, goodness is immediate and evil is mediated. Evil arises from the interposition of something between the self and its own life-affirming instincts. It had been a dreadful mistake (the cliché adjective was the right one) ever to call sin original. Far from being original, it is a perversion. Of course, theologians knew this and said so. The phrase itself, then, was like a Freudian error. It disclosed what was meant even though the rational theological mind denied it. So it was poor doctrine, the lousy result of a theological penchant for paradox.

These thoughts tumbled through his mind. They were ideas he had more or less sorted out in the past. When he began now to think inductively from the starting point of the "sin" in his thighs, he reached a different conclusion.

His mind flashed back to a time in high school or junior high at a swimming party. The girls were perched on the shoulders of the boys like riders astride horses, and the game was to see which rider could throw another off her mount into the water. He had loved the game. In the midst of it he had noticed his mother at the side of the pool, waiting to give him and his friends a lift home in the car. As soon as he and she reached the privacy of their house, she had told him not to play that game again. "A girl should not put that part of her anatomy," she had primly explained, "in touch with a boy's body." He remembered his astonishment at hearing this sentence and how, as she spoke, he could still feel the touch of the girl's thighs on his neck and shoulders. He could not remember how, if at all, he had answered his mother at the time. He knew that inwardly he had rejected her advice, her thought. He knew also that he had been ashamed—partly shamed as she had intended and partly ashamed of her, and of himself for being the son of a prude.

He remembered something else, which he could not date in time, couldn't remember how old he was. It might even have happened more than once. She had told him it wasn't nice for girls or women to sit with their legs apart. Since most of the females he knew didn't often do that (it was before girls took to wearing slacks), this comment made no strong impression, until she went on to add that men should not sit that way either. This had flabbergasted him, for to sit with legs together or crossed meant that the masculine parts between the legs were squeezed, which didn't seem right unless you were trying deliberately to get some sensation there. One sat with legs apart in order that one's crotch could breathe. He didn't say this. He only said, "Why?" She insisted that "spread eagle" was not the posture of a gentleman. He was at the time, whenever it was, some years away from the declaration to her that he was not a gentleman, which disavowal was to make her cry.

There was something wrong about opening your legs. This was the message he accumulated, and while he had never for an instant agreed with it in his mind, nor acquiesced with his conscious will, he knew, had long known, that the message had gotten through. To open his legs was an act of defiance.

He wanted now to walk a fine line. It was not to his purpose to blame any of his hang-ups on his mother. He had gone through that already, and in the course of recent therapy had vented quite a lot of hostility in her direction.

The task now was to assess how he had played the cards life had dealt him, leaving off the childish complaint that the deck was stacked. However, in this very task it was important to see what the cards were. Otherwise, the childish complaint would flip over to its equally childish opposite, the omnipotence fantasy that one dealt one's own cards and could do with them whatever one pleased, as if there were no limits, no finitude, no continuity in the structures of time.

He was sure that the shame was there and that he had not, all on his own, invented it. Nor had his mother. She passed on to him, in the ways characteristic of her, the attitudes she had learned and formed in the course of her life. And he could see, as who could not, that genital shame went back a long way in the human race. You arrived, right soon, at the fig leaves of Adam and Eve. If Original Sin meant that there is a social, historical continuity to the barrier between the self and its instincts, a shame at being oneself, there could be no argument.

What was not valid was to ontologize this, to read it as a curse or a Fall for which there is no remedy except divine intervention from outside of history, like Christ descending from heaven and somehow breaking the bond, and God at the end of time somehow redeeming us from having been born.

How then to acknowledge that sin (self-alienation) is transmitted historically and at the same time not allow it to forbid self-acceptance and praise of life? The answer was in the metaphor of disease. If a doctor has an ill patient, he gets nowhere in his treatment by explaining the history of the

disease. It may comfort the patient to know that others have
had it, that the diagnosis is familiar, that science has thought
about the problem; yet if all this issues in no prescription, it
is cold comfort.

The theologian returned to his disease, not as a concept
but as a feeling. He was sure the way forward was through
the affliction, not around it.

He put his hand once more upon his leg.

They say that the divine antidote for sin is forgiveness. He
thought this wrong, or beside the point. The real point, he
believed, is love. What removes sin is not its being forgiven
but the sinner's being loved. At any rate, he had not to
"forgive" his thighs, much less imagine God would do so.
What they wanted was care, attention, a certain honor—the
opposites of shame, the attitudes of love. His hand resumed
the caress. He opened his nerves to sense what the thigh felt
like. What does my hand find when it touches this flesh?
What is here of attraction and repulsion? He would invite to
consciousness the suppressed sensations. No other way to
love.

The discovery he then made was so simple it surprised
him. He discovered the muscles in the back of his legs.

If at any previous time he had drawn a sketch of the
musculature of his legs, it would have presented a curious
structure. The large muscle group in the front of the thighs
would have been pronounced. So would the calf muscle
and the little ones that move the toes. The knee bones, shin,
ankle, arch, and toe bones would have been clear, as well as
the hip socket. But the muscles running from the back
through the hips and down the rear of the thighs would

have been absent. Even the bone of the thigh would have appeared insignificant. It would have been as if all his control passed in the front of the thigh and then in the rear of the shin to the ankle. Long and graceful as he might have wanted to make this appear, a viewer could not have escaped the impression that he was standing on a most improbable curve, an elongated S.

The muscles in the front of his thighs had never had any pain or given him any trouble. He liked them. They reminded him of his masculinity.

But at the back—or now, in the tub, on the underside—the thigh became soft, feminine, obscure. Or did it? With time at his disposal, and with a resolve to explore, he felt the rear of his thigh first on the surface and then deeper. Probing and grapsing, his touch passed through the fatty tissue and found, beneath, a bundle of muscle.

He came upon it with an astonishment as great as if he were standing upon a peak in Darien. "Well, I'll be God damned," he said.

He moved the right leg to see what these muscles were for. He hadn't the faintest notion. He was to find later, interviewing his friends, that other people didn't know either. But it was fortunate he did not yet know how widely his ignorance was shared, for that might have abated his curiosity. He found that the muscles in the rear of the thigh contract when the leg is extended, and that they contracted most of all, became very firm, when he kicked down hard with his heel. He performed this exercise several times, and as he did so he was overtaken by a shock of recognition.

Several old pieces of knowledge he had not previously

been able to integrate or use gathered at once. He had to separate them in order to think. The first had to do with his frequent anger.

The theologian had a strong temper. When he was angry his energy would rise to the top of his body. His eyes became fierce, even wild, his voice rapid, loud, and eloquent; his face was flushed, neck rigid, fists clenched and moving in gestures emanating mainly from the elbows. His shoulders did not much get into the act. If he was very angry, he would sometimes kick with his feet in fast, short jabs. At the end of such an outburst he was invariably reduced to tears.

This violent temper, which was said to be frightening to behold and which seemed to him so at odds with the character of a teacher, theologian, and man of faith, had been the occasion for much therapy in the past. He had learned from reading Rollo May that his anger was a *daemon*, a part of himself for which he tended to take no responsibility and which therefore turned against him, making him its principal victim. He knew that he was not in possession of his anger, that he refused to own and possess it. The more he treated it like an affliction or a visitation of some evil spirit, the worse it got. So he had for some time now consciously affirmed this anger, regarding it as one of his own attributes, and it had become less threatening and less frequent.

He realized now that the change in his mental attitude, very good as far as it went, was less than whole because it had not included a transformation in the subjectivity of his body. It was, he thought, like a Christian conversion not consummated by baptism.

His anger, which was nothing if not a bodily response to

some situation or other, whatever else it might also be—his anger, which was a deed done, or usually half done, could not be transformed at the mental level only. It wanted a full psychosomatic integration. He came to this conviction not by theoretical deduction from premises, though in truth he had been doing some reading along this line. What convinced him now was the involuntary experience of anger when he flexed the muscles in the rear of his thigh. He was not conscious of any outer condition or person to make him angry now. On the contrary, the bath, the hour, the solitude were most pleasing to him. Yet the extension of the leg and the thrusting of the heel, with his attention devoted to the behavior of the thigh muscles in this action, put him in immediate touch with an objectless anger. He felt it in the pit of his stomach. "God damn!" he said.

He flashed back to a mountain hike he had taken with friends two years ago. It was the clearest former occasion he knew of the rise in him of an anger he could find no excuse for blaming on anyone or anything but himself. Everyone was pleasant, the day fine, the mountain one he had long wanted to explore and not particularly difficult. Yet as he climbed he had become almost beside himself with anger. He had tried like the devil to find some slightest pretext in the company for venting his anger upon them, was quite aware of doing so, but they had given him no excuse, and he had had to realize that the anger was of his own making. It came to him now with a start that in climbing the mountain he would have made vigorous use of these muscles at the back of his thighs, though that would not have occurred to him when he climbed because then he did not even know that he had such muscles. The anger was the discharge (however uneconomical) of an energy not integrated into the climb because his body and his mind were at war in the region of his thigh. Every exertion of that muscle group required an effort of blocking its awareness from consciousness. So, in addition to the energy needed for climbing, other energies were needed to carry on an internal war, to distract himself from identifying with the very muscles that were doing most of work. This internal war was a closed system. Its fraction of his total energy could not flow outward. Frustrated, this closed-circuit energy looked for an outlet, like an electric current looking for ground. If only there were something out there to strike! Or better, to kick. The anger looked for an object, but he was too rational that day to find it, his friends too oblivious of his mood to cooperate. Needless to say, he reached the top of the mountain as exhausted as he was frustrated. His mood was then "dumpy" and "grumpy." They noticed that and decided wisely to pay no attention. He had not climbed a mountain since that day.

Now, in the tub, he began to think on his anger at home. It was clear to him that when he blew his stack at wife or kids he invoked everything at his command except his larger muscles. Of the very strong muscles in his body he was conscious of using in anger only those of the jaw and the neck, which he clenched, though he did not actually bite anybody except once. These muscles are among the strongest in the body, but they are not the largest. The really large muscles are those of the shoulders, upper arms, abdomen, back, and thighs. None of these was conspicuous in his anger. It was as if the anger was projected to the extremities of his body, evacuating the major centers of power and feeling. His tongue would let fly with words: the tongue of a serpent, rapid, volatile, wounding with venom. His eyes would flash fire. The jaw, loose and agile when talking, would in silence become a fortress. The arms flailed mostly from the elbows, fists moving like big weights at the end of sticks. His legs, if they got into the act at all, were used from the knees downward. Perhaps one knee would be drawn up as a weapon, and the foot might fly outward in a jab of sudden swiftness. The skin surface, all over, was highly charged with feeling. To touch it at such a time was to risk attack by an electric fan.

Frightful as all this was, it was also most curious. Had it ever been observed by a totally disinterested party, it would have seemed comic. He became as brittle as a marionnette while pretending to the emotions of King Lear. You might be very afraid of what he would do next, but you could not be afraid of *him*, because in a curious way he was not there. "He's not all there," a bystander might have thought. His wife thought, as the saying goes, that he was beside himself, which he was.

It was conceivable that he held back the use of his large muscles during angry moments because he didn't want to hurt anybody. Was this partial noninvolvement a way of restraining a lethal rage? Possibly. Or possibly that was the genesis of the pattern some time in infancy or childhood. But he thought of something more likely. He was not conscious of his mother's ever restraining him from killing anybody or even from hurting them physically, because he had not been given to such behavior. But he was very conscious of her attempts to restrain his feelings. For one reason or another, he had let her do it, in part at least. In this, society had been her ally, or she its agent. Another ally, the strongest of all, had been religion.

When he thought of his religious upbringing, in spite of the fact that he was raised as a southern Methodist, one of the more emotional brands of middle-class Protestantism, he remembered it mostly as an inhibition of feeling. Methodism, as he had known it, was very good at training your attitudes, but it did so at the expense of your feelings. That is, it asked for the inculcated attitudes to be felt (he had heard plenty about John Wesley's heart-warming and about the testimony of inward conviction), but it did not encourage you to let spontaneous feelings influence your attitudes. And of all the spontaneous feelings it seemed to discourage, the chief was anger, even more than sex. Worse than in its sexual prudery, Methodism came across to him, even today, as prudish about anger, hostility, and all the negative feelings.

It is hard enough to control one's own feelings, let alone somebody else's. There is only one way to do it, never wholly successful, praise God: to rigidify or deaden the body. He remembered those afternoon naps, obligatory when he was a preschool child. He could not be made to sleep, but he could be forced to remain still by threat of punishment for any sound of stirring. He wondered if his legs had ever been held down to prevent their thrashing about in anger, hunger, or something. He didn't know. He remembered a fight with his brother, unfinished because of maternal interference, when he had shouted, "I hate him,

and he hates me!" To which she replied, "That's not true."
It was not that remark that had inhibited his feelings, because he knew what he felt then and there better than she
did. The restraint was her removing him physically from
the fight, standing him in front of her chair till the feelings
went down instead of out through his fists and legs. And
when he was naughty to Johnny Huddle or to the old lady
called Mrs. Snot-nose who lived down the street, he had to
get dressed up in nice clothes and go with his mother to
stand at their front door and mumble some sort of apology,
his body hardly daring even to tremble with the rage he
was afraid to let himself feel. Hold your breath. Make small
motions only. Be a nice little man (translation: a stick on a
string). Control your temper.

Maybe it was good for him, who knows? Nevertheless, it
would have to be undone.

"And how is the good boy today?" John Pierrakos was
talking, but the tone (if not the exact words) was that of his
mother, whom John could imitate without ever having
met. The question paralyzed. The puppet answered, he
couldn't remember what.

Pierrakos was his therapist, a year or so before the
bathtub.

Pierrakos had noticed that the theologian had an obstruc-
tion or block in the thighs. He would observe the theologian's posture and the way his body behaved in motion.
One day he had put his fingers around the thigh and said,
"It's as if there were a tourniquet here." The theologian had
not replied to that. He remembered thinking, is that so? So
what? He hated the instruction to lie down on the couch and

kick, but he always obeyed it like a good boy. Pierrakos clearly hoped that he would one day get angry during their hour and kick off the good boy behavior, but he had never done so.

The only time he was truly angry with Pierrakos was when the therapist kept him waiting forty-five minutes for his appointment. Noticing the eyes full of anger, Pierrakos handed him a bataka (a baseball bat made of foam rubber), and he had flailed the tardy therapist with all his might. That felt so good he thought it worth the price of admission to all the months of therapy. But he had never, not even then, felt anger in his legs. So it was not quite true to say that he had swung the bat with all his might. "Whatsoever your hand finds to do . . ." He remembered the quotation. And he remembered Kierkegaard's line: "Purity of heart is to will one thing."

Gemini had never had a pure heart. Was that why he had chosen to be a theologian and an actor and a drama critic? He had pretty much given up the critic's role. He believed that the task of the theologian, like that of the actor, was to go beyond split consciousness, to find, in a lifetime of work, purity of heart beneath one's mask.

Pierrakos noticed also the theologian's feet, and what he said about them wounded the patient's narcissism as deeply as anything ever had. He said that the arches were too high.

Now, the theologian prided himself for being light on his feet. He thought that the high arch of his foot was graceful. It more than made up for any inferiority he might feel when people, especially shoe salesmen, noticed that his feet were small. Big men have big feet, and he certainly wanted to be a big man. But he scorned flat-footed people, as he scorned flat-footed statements. He was proud of his arched foot, of the arched comments he could make, and of his whole sense of being able to maneuver like Hermes. His fantasy, which he'd never told anyone, was that he was a messenger from the gods. It was the redeeming side of his being a theologian, otherwise a ponderous calling. He detested reading most theologians because their style was flat.

And Pierrakos said his arches were too high. Couldn't the poor fellow notice their grace?

Still, he had enough grace to ask why, and promptly found out. Pierrakos had noticed not simply the feet but also their relation to the whole body. He noticed the size of the body frame, the height of five eleven or so, and the weight of some one hundred seventy pounds; and he said that the acute arch of the foot on a body of such a size suggested that the weight was not being given fully to the ground.

It belonged to the therapy they were doing to stress the "grounding" of one's body and psyche. The theologian liked this metaphor. It made physical sense. It fit with the cycles of nature. It was intelligible in terms of electric circuitry, not to mention the gravitational field. It had an ancient history and tied in with things he was reading in mythology. And it reminded him of Paul Tillich's phrase for God: "the ground of Being."

But the theologian was a sky person. He was Hermes at heart. He had arched and tender feet, and for him grounding was not easy. There was even lurking in him the aviator's negative sense of the phrase, to be grounded.

Had it not been for his anger, for those flights of rage in

his life, so clearly disfunctional, maybe sinful, he would not have taken the notion of grounding so seriously. He simply could not escape the truth of it when Pierrakos spoke to him in the following way, saying, "You fight like someone not sure of his ground."

Lack of adequate grounding was manifest also in the theologian's voice. Like his arches, his voice tended to be too high, missing the full resonance his chest and head might have supplied. His speaking often revealed inflections of pleading, as if he were not himself quite sure of the ground he took.

That one's voice has a connection to the ground had not occurred to Hermes. Had he been well trained as a singer, or better trained as an actor, he would have known it. Intuition also would have told him had he not rejected his thighs and the awareness that comes through them, but this knowledge had remained hidden until the ceremony of the bathtub.

He had learned somewhere along the way that voice production begins in the region of the pubic bone. Such was his hermetic isolation from the ground that knowledge of the pubic origin of one's voice had not caused him to think downward. Instead, he thought only of the voice rising through the body cavity, over the vocal cords, out the mouth and into the air. He did not even ponder the physical principle that an energy moving in one direction requires an equal and opposite force in the other. The furthest down he had ever thought about voice was when he had discovered, maybe three years before, that to hit and sustain a high note while singing hymns in church, it helped if he relaxed his anus. He felt a bit dirty, perhaps subversive of worship, to have made this discovery in church. But church was the only place he ever sang much, and he rationalized the matter by thinking that if it made the hymns sound better to the ears of almighty God then it was justified. Even so, he was troubled by his lingering impression that people in church had no business having anuses, much less allowing them to open. What if this became public knowledge? What if the minister should invite the congregation to open their anuses and sing? He comforted himself with remembrance of Martin Luther's scatological mind and wondered what Luther thought about in church.

The theologian and the therapist had worked many months on grounding. It was good work, and he probably would not have begun, certainly not finished, the bathtub ceremony without it. But the therapy had not, while it was going on, uncovered the obliviated muscles in the rear of the thighs of both legs.

Again now he flexed his legs, one at a time. As he did so—this was hard to explain—he allowed himself to "go with" them. To tauten the rear thigh muscles, he thrust his heels out. It would have been usual for him, making such a gesture, to push the heels *away* from himself, as if they were some kind of patrol or missile sent out beyond the statutory limit of his *persona*. Now he made consciously an act of identification. "*I* stiffen, *I* extend, *I* push against the tub." He went down into his legs and heels.

He was in for a further surprise. In the aftermath of this movement a flood of feeling rolled upward in his body. It started in the heels as they touched the hard and cold porcelain of the tub. Then it traveled up his legs as a warmth of sensation. It flooded the whole of his thighs and from there spread into his groin and lower abdomen. The whole region was alive with feeling, and so excited was he by this vibrancy that his back tingled and shivered. He tilted his head backward and opened his mouth wide, pushing hard with his heel and feeling on his face a wide, open-mouthed grin. He exhaled strongly and relaxed into the water. He could not remember a time when he was more at one with himself.

For the first time in more than an hour he put weight on his legs. He drew them under him and got first onto his knees. He rocked like this for a few moments. Then he moved his feet under him and squatted, letting his tail dip in the water. He felt the weight of his torso on his thighs, and the weight of all on his feet, his ankles stretched and supple in the balance. Then he began to stand.

He came up slowly. It was important to follow the burden of his weight as it was lifted by those muscles in the thighs. He realized with a start that these were the muscles needed to get him to an upright position. The symbolism of that was staggering. He was a man who, quite literally, had not known how he got himself up. He resisted following out the symbolism. That was for later. Now it was more important to notice the muscles do their job. He felt them contract, wishing he knew more about the mechanics of their attachment and the collaboration, the reciprocal arrangement of those in front and those in back. But he went with what knowledge he had. He felt the weight push down and the muscles pull so that the bone took the weight, and the firmness came into the back of his thighs and then the calves, and he felt the push of his feet against the bottom of the tub, and then he was nearly straight up, and he pushed through his thighs to his heels, and his head was erect and he was looking out the window at the strong light of day on distant hills.

He lifted his left leg and stepped out onto the floor. Then the other leg, and reached for a towel. The linoleum of the floor was cool and soft. He dried first his thighs, massaging the backs of them and feeling the muscle under the fat. His legs felt new. While there was plenty of fat and he had to stand with his feet wide apart to dry the inner softness, still each thigh had more muscle than he had supposed. As he bent and rubbed, he could feel the muscle working to maintain his balance and to give mobility to his back.

He finished drying and went into the bedroom. The whole house seemed still asleep, and his wife had not stirred. He put on his clothes and went downstairs. At the kitchen door, as he opened it, he was met by the gigantic Labrador pup, agitated from head to tail, avid for company, excitement, and the freedom of the out of doors. It did not bark, but it scampered and breathed so loud that he ssh'shed it not to rouse the sleepers awake. He put on some water for coffee and went with the dog outside.

He could not tell if he was more fascinated by the earth beneath his feet or by the radiance of the morning light. The dog ran in the manner of random spirit such animals display when they know not which attraction to follow. He watched it lift its thigh to piss at least a score of times.

He was drawn to the flower garden. It was carefully but not primly cultivated. It was a square rimmed by a low stone wall. The center was grass, and the beds occupied the four sides. Everything was lush green, and the peonies, marigolds, and a few other June bloomers were speaking in color. There were tiny droplets of dew. He stood in the middle and looked at each flower and leaf.

Praise is not quite the word for what he felt. The word obscures the keen perception of his sight. Communion is a better word, though still too pious. He was conscious of a deep transaction between himself and the place where he stood. He and the flowers both sent down roots. He was not sure but that his were deeper than theirs. Still, he had no desire to make invidious comparisons. This thought put him on to what he meant. We send down the roots that we need. The earth receives our search for an adequate grounding.

He had not, until today, put down deep roots. Figuratively, yes. But the body is not a figure, though it may cut one, and the self is not a type. We put down the roots that we need. In the maturity of his life the symbols had proved too shallow. He wanted to go deeper. He wanted the firmer soil of the literal truth. Symbols, he knew, grew from the deep. If not, they withered. The God he believed in was not a symbol. God was the deep from which the symbols grew. Last night his friend has said, "There are earth mothers and sky fathers. We need some earth fathers."

His foot pressed the soil. His thigh pushed it there. He inhaled. He turned toward the house, the dog frolicking after him. The other dog barked inside the house. His friends would be up. He walked on his earth father-mother toward the house. The symbols fell away. Neither father nor mother would emblem what he felt. He was full of an energy that has no name.

Dear Tillich: To Be or Not To Be Is Not the Question

Y O U taught me so much I tremble to take issue with the concept dearest to your mind. I have taken a long time even to start thinking about it. No teacher I ever had was as liberating as you. With passionate philosophical love, you approached Christian revelation to find out what it *means*. This was my question, too, and that of the multitudes whom you addressed. I became your disciple, welcomed you as my theological father. Twenty years went by before I dared controvert you in public, and by that time you had passed over the great divide.

The pages of the book in which I publish this letter will show how much I am still under your sway. That will be so, I think, to the end of my days. But there is protest, too. I must come out with this or fail to walk on my own theological legs. The fact is, dear Tillich, I have become disenchanted with Being.

Here I can see you put the letter down and turn your gaze

to the sun of eternal truth that no doubt shines where you are. I remember how much you liked sunsets. I once stood beside you on a top floor of the RCA building while you, enraptured by the sun setting beyond Manhattan and the Hudson, ignored everything the RCA man was excitedly telling you about his recent trip to Moscow. I wonder whether, in the place you now are, the sun of truth rises and sets. Wallace Stevens has asked my question for me:

> Is there no change . . . in paradise?
> Does ripe fruit never fall?[1]

I have started on a quest for a theology of *doing*. I have fallen in love with patterns of actions, which are called *gestalts*. I remember your phrase, "Gestalts of grace," and I have paraphrased it in the title of this book. (How's that for ambivalence?) I have decided that "Being" will not do justice to the action involved in the formation of patterns, nor to the dynamic role they play in our lives. I have returned to my old love of theater, poetry, and stories and have been seduced again by Aristotle to think of these as "imitations of action." I have decided that the most important words are verbs and that "Being" is too weak and vague a verb to "imitate" the action of God, or any action. For me, "Being" has come to obscure, not enlighten, the patterns of grace, and the graciousness of the patterns. So I am writing you some of my thought to help make it clearer to me, if not to you. I start with nouns and verbs.

Edwin Muir wrote a poem I like called "The Incarnate

---

[1] "Sunday Morning," from *The Collected Poems of Wallace Stevens* (New York: Alfred A. Knopf, 1955), p. 69.

One." Muir was a Scotsman, and the poem is a protest against Scottish Calvinism. I realize you may think it has little to do with a Lutheran Rhinelander and *bon vivant* like yourself, but I start with it anyway because it includes a theological protest I share:

The windless northern surge, the sea-gull's scream,
And Calvin's kirk crowning the barren brae.
I think of Giotto the Tuscan shepherd's dream,
Christ, man and creature in their inner day.
How could our race betray
The Image, and the Incarnate One unmake
Who chose this form and fashion for our sake?

The Word made flesh here is made word again,
A word made word in flourish and arrogant crook.
See there King Calvin with iron pen,
And God three angry letters in a book,
And there the logical hook
On which the Mystery is impaled and bent
Into an ideological instrument.

.   .   .

The fleshless word, growing, will bring us down,
Pagan and Christian man alike will fall,
The auguries say, the white and black and brown,
The merry and sad, theorist, lover, all
Invisibly will fall:
Abstract calamity, save for those who can
Build their cold empire on the abstract man.[2]

.   .   .

[2] Edwin Muir, *One Foot in Eden* (New York: Grove Press, 1956), p. 47.

I hope you like the poem's smiling reference to Giotto, a favorite of yours you taught me to love. Then I hope you won't be too furious when I say I think the great concept, Being, has become a "logical hook" and an "ideological instrument." In fact, I think it always was. And I think it has served, even in your sophisticated use of it, to help bring about the "abstract calamity" that has befallen both Christianity and culture in our time.

My hope is to bring theology to battle against "the abstract man." The first task is to beef up theological language, because it has too many nouns and not enough verbs. The nouns are the prodigious offspring of "Being," which is their abstract father. I'm going to go looking for verbs and their down-to-earth mother, too long kept in the back of the theological house.

What must theology do to be saved? It must enter a second time into its mother's womb and be born. When Nicodemus asked incredulously how he could do that, he was not as dense as some people think. True, he betrayed a rather literal mind; but if one's imagination does not instantly soar, the literal offers the best path to follow. If theological imagination today has become weak, which seems to me the case, theology can do worse than to ask about its mother's womb—to inquire, that is, into the natural order of fecundity out of which it first sprang. For it will not be heretical—and even if it were, that would not matter—to suggest that the second birth is of the same parentage as the first, even though in the second all is translated into spiritual power.

The womb out of which theology came, as you, dear Tillich, well knew, is prerational, ecstatic, and fluid. It has many names. For some, it is called Revelation. For Rudolf Otto, whom you so admired, it was the numinous, the holy. Thomas Fawcett has recently called it "symbolic awareness." For Carl Jung, though I do not agree with him, it is the store of primordial archetypes in the collective unconscious. It is the same, or nearly the same, as poetic imagination.

By whatever name she is known, this mother stands to theology in that ambivalent relation in which a natural mother stands to her child: she was and remains the creative womb from which its life proceeds, while at the same time she is that which the child strives unceasingly to surpass. In the present instance, if I do not somehow reveal the poetic spring of my thought you will reject it as a lifeless exercise, while if I were to offer you only a poem, even a good one, you would conclude that I had not spoken theologically.

The reason so many of us have not well understood the relation of theology to literature is that both disciplines have seduced us into a veritable idolatry of words. Each of them alone has the seductive power to do this. Literature seems to be the art of the arrangement of words. Theology, in addition to being wordy, contains in its Christian form a doctrine of the primacy of Word in Creation and Redemption. Taken together, literature and theology may tempt us into thinking that heaven and earth are made out of language. "In the beginning was the Word." We speak glibly of a literary world, so called; and as theologians we seem to inhabit a theological world. All this is dangerous.

The theological doctrine of the Word, I fear, has preened itself into an outrageous male chauvinism. No woman would ever have invented such a doctrine, much less allowed it to go to her head. We need to recover our senses. The literary imagination should be the primary witness among us to "that which is too deep for words."

Rational discourse tends to move from the concrete to the abstract. When I look at this tendency with the aid of philology, I observe a passage from verbs to nouns. The phenomenon was well noticed by Ernest Fenollosa in an essay on "The Chinese Written Character as a Medium for Poetry."[3] "A true noun, an isolated thing," he writes, "does not exist in nature. Things are . . . the meeting points of actions, cross-sections cut through actions, snap-shots. Neither can a pure verb, an abstract motion, be possible in nature. The eye sees noun and verb as one: things in motion, motion in things."[4] Even so, the verb has a certain primacy because it is the motion, the change, the *difference made* that attracts attention. Fenollosa suggests, and I agree, that the sentence form arises in all languages because it reflects the temporal order of natural sequences. "All truth," he says, "is the *transference of power*."[5] From this arises the sentence

[3] Reprinted in *Prose Keys to Modern Poetry*, ed. Karl Shapiro (New York: Harper & Row, 1962), pp. 136–154. The essay was written shortly before Fenollosa died in 1908. It had much influence on Ezra Pound. I am told that some authorities on Chinese think Fenollosa got it wrong, and I have left that part out. Be that as it may, he is right about perception and about Shakespeare. (See below.)

[4] *Ibid.*, p. 141.

[5] *Ibid.*, p. 142. Author's italics.

form: subject, verb, object. The verb stands for a certain transference of power from subject to object. Action is the essence of a sentence, which is why we were taught at school that no sentence is complete without a verb.

The function of verbs is to represent the activities that we recognize—that is, respond to—in our environment. Nouns represent only certain arbitrary fixed points at the termini or at the intersections of actions. "Almost all the Sanskrit roots," Fenollosa tells us, "are primitive verbs." Even the English word *is* comes from an Aryan root meaning "to breathe." The various parts of speech, which can never be fully codified, are extrapolations from a more primitive way of speaking in which action is all. This is still the language of the street. Fenollosa says in witty rhetoric, "Nounizing is itself an abstraction."[6]

If we turn to poetry, we find Fenollosa's observations marvelously corroborated. He himself turned to Shakespeare:

I had to discover for myself [he says] why Shakespeare's English was so immeasurably superior to all others. I found that it was his persistent, natural, and magnificent use of hundreds of transitive verbs. Rarely will you find an "is" in his sentences. "Is" weakly lends itself to the uses of our rhythm, in the unaccented syllables; yet he sternly discards it. A study of Shakespeare's verbs should underlie all exercises in style.[7]

The poet differs from the writer of prose by shaping language to express action. Not only does the poet use more

---

[6] *Prose Keys,* pp. 146, 145.
[7] *Ibid.,* p. 152.

verbs, but also he or she awakens the verbal tone of the other parts of speech. Often the poet musters nouns to march as verbs.

I've been reading what Kenneth Koch wrote about teaching small school children on New York's lower West Side to write poems. Here's a specimen of what was produced, which I hope may amuse you and which shows what I mean about getting nouns to behave like verbs. It was written by a certain Charles Conroy in the fifth grade.

> Oh green, yellow, orange, pink, red, black, brown,
> What shall I chartreuse today?
> I could chartreuse with brown and gold,
> Or I could red John in the nose. What could I
>   chartreuse?
> I put a green croak in Pinky's bed, what shall I
>   chartruese?
> I could put a silver yeow on teacher's chair
> What shall I chartreuse?
> I could ooze the blue toothpaste in Dad's face.
>   What shall I chartreuse?
> What could I chartreuse if I got a paint brush?
> Oh, oh I just wasted the day on thinking on what
>   I shall chartreuse
> But I could always think of something to crown
>   yellow tomorrow.[8]

Imagine old Van Gogh, whom we both love, going

[8] Kenneth Koch and the Students of P.S. 61 in New York City, *Wishes, Lies, and Dreams: Teaching Children to Write Poetry* (New York: Vintage Books, 1970), p. 210.

around yellowing everything! And swirling the light. And chopping space to glory.

Action is also the secret of the poet's figures of speech, over which metaphor reigns. Samuel Taylor Coleridge said that a metaphor reconciles opposites. Cleanth Brooks taught that the good metaphor is "paradoxical," which is to approach it by way of logic and thus come to a halt. Brooks and Wimsatt hit closer when they spoke of the metaphor's "tension." But that is still too mechanical for me, and I have called it a form of "intercourse," taking my cue from Wallace Stevens and, latterly, from Norman O. Brown. In class, I have excited students by teaching them to notice that a good metaphor "oscillates" or "shimmers." Even Erich Neumann, the priest of archetypes, says that "the symbol intimates, suggests, excites."[9]

The metaphor, we may say, expresses what Fenollosa saw the sentence-form to express: a transference of power. Yet there is a difference. The sentence typically does it in the temporal sequence of subject-verb-object. It will say "Man bites dog." The metaphor shows the transference of power running in two directions at once. The man who bites the dog is a dog-man, not to say a mad-dog-man, while the bitten dog is a man-dog, no doubt getting mad. Here *change* has become *exchange*. With such traffic is metaphor always employed. Nothing lives or dies but does suffer a sea-change. Such is the maxim of poetry, the language of all people closely in touch with life.

[9] *The Great Mother* (New York: Pantheon Books, 1955), p. 17.

Dear Tillich, I hope this hasn't been too boring so far. I can hear you grumble that it's all very obvious and doesn't have much to do with philosophy or theology. Maybe. Let me venture on. I'm going to say something with which I know you won't agree but which I'm coming to think anyhow. Somewhere along the line philosophy took on the task of squelching the verbs. Up through Heraclitus there was too much flux. With Parmenides, philosophy set out to reduce the flux to something that did not move. The result was "Being," the denominator of the unchanging aspect of everything.

The basis of the demand for something permanent—that is, for an ontic substratum—was not only logical. (Logic came late.) Nature herself asks for structure. So, the relative of an amoeba will grow bones and become a vertebrate, perhaps even a fossil. There is nothing wrong with finding structures and seeking out permanence *unless:* unless these "fixities and definites" (Coleridge) be denonimated "the real." When this is done, we get the inverted propositon that the static points are more nearly real than the actions they qualify. As if a train were the engine, cars, and track rather than the motion of the thing. This error is by now embedded in our language. The very word *real* means "like things." In other words, what we call the real is already an abstraction, because things are abstractions. The term *reality*, by which we set so much store, is a noun made from an adjective made from a noun: it retains hardly a trace of action.

Philosophy's biggest blow to all actions was to take the weakest, most omnipresent verb in the language, the copula, and turn it into a noun, which philosophy then used as the name of the most universal category of thought, as well as the predicate of all existence. I wonder if you know a witty essay about this by Eugen Rosenstock-Huessy which takes the form of a letter supposedly written by Heraclitus to Parmenides.[10] It was bad enough, though perhaps tolerable, Heraclitus says, when nouns were turned into pronouns. Parmenides, the father of ontology, has now taken the further step of turning a verb into a pro-verb. Instead of thundering, Zeus now "has being." Instead of hunting, Artemis "participates in being." The gods are thus either robbed of their actions entirely or else find their deeds subsumed under the presumably higher category of Being, which retains, at most, only the ghost or pale shadow of action.

I agree with Rosenstock-Huessy's Heraclitus that this simply won't do, and for the plain reason that a god apart from his action is nothing. Rosenstock-Huessy has Heraclitus to say that, "Their acts are the only facts known of the Gods. We see them in their acts first and never see much more of them" (p. 85). I should go further and say we never see *any* more of them, because there is nothing more to be seen. Zeus is the name of thundering. It is true that Zeus is not reducible to thunder because Zeus also loves, begets, rules and does other things. It does not follow that there is an essence, Zeus, who is abstractable from these activities, much less that the activities are mere reflections of his attributes.

---

[10] Eugen Rosenstock-Huessy, *I am an Impure Thinker* (Norwich, Vermont: Argo Books, 1970), pp. 77–90.

The same is true of the One God of Israel, Yahweh, who is said recently to have died. At any rate to die is better than merely to be, for at least something happens. As I see it, however, the so-called death of the so-called God occurs simultaneously with the bankruptcy of Western abstractionism. A God who is Being Itself, which is quite indistinguishable from no being at all, or a God who is so Wholly Other that his actions are but the caprice of His left hand, a God who has *aseity* or pure in-himself-ness, is hard put to die, being so near that condition already. When we heard of his death, we responded as did Dorothy Parker when told that Calvin Coolidge had died: "How can they tell?"

I know that you were very upset by Thomas Altizer and some other death-of-God theologians who tried to say they were following your footsteps. I know that your whole aim was to *prevent* the death of God and to show that God is a *living* God. I know that you feared that a finite God *would* die, so you bent every effort to make it clear that God is the *ground* or *source* of life. I know this, and I agreed with you. Nevertheless the divine patient started gasping. After the funeral, I decided (forgive me) that you had administered the wrong medicine.

The so-called dead God is a casualty of dying abstractions. Almost all Western thought suffers from creeping paralysis of the categories. We have a culture so cut off from nature that if a leaf stirs this culture hardly knows what it is seeing and has to rush to explain the phenomenon by static categories either scientific or philosophical. When we are done, the leaf has *not* stirred. That was only a figure of speech.

It is to your great credit as an ontologist, dear Tillich, to have remembered that actionless Being is the same as nothing and to have attempted, therefore, to pump action back into the very term invented to get rid of it. Thus, you tried to understand Being as the *Power* of Being. This is why the feminist theologian Mary Daly got so excited by your theology, which provided a lively relief from the Thomism she had been used to. Her feminist manifesto, *Beyond God the Father*, has a lyric Tillichian chapter called "God the Verb." The verb, of course, which is almost your *only* verb, is Being.

It was a valiant effort on your part and hers to try to make Being into a healthy verb. Old Heidegger was in there pitching, too. But the effort is bound to fail, as I guess my own feebler and different approach will, too. However, if I am going to fail I may as well do it my way.

To the Power of Being you gave two main functions. The first was the power to overcome Non-Being. The struggle between Being and Non-Being, by which the positive power took the negative into itself without being destroyed was the "dialectic of Being." This gave Being something to *do*: to assert itself courageously over the threat of nothingness or chaos. The trouble, as you realized, is that this boils down to an eternal back-and-forth between Yes and No, which can go on forever without getting anywhere.

Out of yes *versus* no comes no pattern. You had therefore to say that the step "from essence to existence" (the creation of the world) cannot be derived from the Power of Being. It is, you said, "a story to be told." That's right. And I'm saying that the preamble about Being and Non-Being is beside the point. The story should begin where the story does begin—with the first action. That's where the Book of Genesis starts, and with much wisdom. Of course, it's a myth. You always had the philosopher's desire to get behind myth. I sometimes wish I could do so myself, but I have decided I cannot. I have decided God cannot, either. The only way to get behind a myth is to go abstract. Then the show is over, and all the characters, including God, have disappeared.

The second role you gave to the Power of Being was to sustain in being everything that exists as long as it does exist. That sounds good, but there are problems with it. In the first place, it assumes the inexplicable transition or step from essence to existence, the very act that Being, as such, cannot account for. If Being, as Being, doesn't necessarily or intelligibly *make* anything, then how in the name of heaven does it *sustain* anything? These verbs are out of place. By starting with Being, we have cut ourselves off from all specific actions that make a difference between this, that, and the other. Starting from Being, anything at all may happen, except that the one thing that may not happen is *nothing*. Your famous "ontological question" was, "Why is there something and not nothing?" Well, I'm sure I don't know. And neither do you. Certainly the concept of Being does not answer it. Not even the Power of Being.

I have come to think, dear Tillich, that it is foolish to ask *why* about most things, and certainly about *all* things. Your question, "Why is there something and not nothing" is really an exclamation: "Oh, the world *is*!" Now that's fine. I share its feeling. I am ever and again astonished that when I open my eyes I *see*. "Fresh every morning," as the song puts it. I hope never to outgrow the astonishment the world evokes from me. But I do hope to outgrow asking *why*. The only answer is, "Because . . ." You can put Being in the blanks or any word you like. It changes nothing. What does make a difference is to ask *what*. What am I seeing? What does it do? What do I feel? What will I do next? This is the drama, and I do not think we can get behind it without statements so vague they are meaningless.

If I am told, by A. N. Whitehead for instance, that the very purpose of a metaphysical statement is to enunciate a general condition that applies equally to all phenomena, I reply, like a good pragmatist, that such a statement can have no operative function, no "cash-value," as William James would say.

These thoughts in mind, I have come up with something—I beg your pardon, and also that of William James, who deserves the credit—I call "Driver's law." It says, "That which makes no difference cannot be known." Conversely, whatever is known makes a difference. The corollary is that acts, changes, occurrences are all that can be known. A steady state, a pure essence, if indeed it were steady, would be as destructive for knowledge and thought-process as the famous "black box" of psychological experimenters. There can be, strictly speaking, no metaphysics of process because process cannot be subordinated to an absolute or wholly general idea. The same is true of a metaphysics or ontology of life. What makes life life is surprise, novelty, unaccountable freedom. There are structures, too. But what makes life life is the freedom of the structures. You made this latter point well in the third volume of your *Systematic Theology*, but it is a point that cannot be taken from Being as such. We are back to stories that have to be told.

Dear Tillich, I have decided to let go of the question of being. Neither in you nor in Shakespeare is it the question of interest.

Hamlet's "To be or not to be," is the question of a man fleeing his destiny. It is the flight, not the abstract possibility of flight, with which Shakespeare could and did deal. Likewise human thought, action, and theology can deal with flight only in its occurrence, not with its sheer essence. I do not need a theory of flight in order to discern that a man is running, and I do not need a theory of Non-Being to explain that things come and go.

Paul Ricoeur was on the right track when he said that "the symbol gives rise to thought." This formula makes it clear that rational reflection depends upon the symbol, not the other way around. But what gives rise to the symbol?

Concern for the genesis of image and symbol, much more than for their abstract flower, dominates the literary mind, as it should the theological mind also. Your poet, your creator of literature, cares little what symbols mean, is irritable if you ask. Literary interest lies in creation, not cryptology. Only your pedant, your academic, in a few cases your odd genius like James Joyce, will write in order to be deciphered. Your true poet knows that the secret of images lies in their origins, writes poems to celebrate their birth. A symbol is an image loaded with associations such that a whole range of experience is unified. The unification is not achieved by any magical power inherent in the symbol. The power of a symbol is that of a certain charge. Like a battery, a symbol can go dead from nonuse or overuse. The power of a symbol is derived from the experiential acts that are represented in it. A symbol is a storehouse of energy. A philosopher, theologian, or poet who handles symbols well is concerned with their stored energy.

An image is the precipitate of an encounter between the human being and some part of the environment. In other words, an image is a *gestalt*. It is the form an encounter has taken in the mind of one or more of the interacting subjects. If a poet writes a poem about a tree, he has to avoid letting the poem be a catalog of stock images that are the residue of other tree-encounters than his own. A bad poet will have had no such encounter, and the poem will at best be the clever manipulation of stock images. The good poet will avoid poems about trees unless he has an experience sufficiently unique to call forth a new, or newly modified, image of the subject. We recognize the good poem by its plasticity to the experience that gave it rise. This criterion applies equally to the poem that is simple and to the one that is complex.

I have noticed two characteristics of experiences that give rise to poetry. The first is that they are always actions; that is to say, transactions. Whatever remains passive or static in a poem is not yet poetry. Poetry has to do only with what is alive. In poetry, even death is not dead.

The second characteristic is this: experience is always intersubjective, even in the case of a poem written about *nature* and *things* rather than about people. As poetry has only to do with what is alive, so it has only to do with what meets, addresses, and listens to the poet.

Taught to watch out for the "pathetic fallacy," we nowadays are usually willing to say only that a poet can sometimes get away with a certain amount of empathy. So we might read, for instance, the lines of Wallace Stevens:

> One must have a mind of winter
> To regard the frost and the boughs
> Of the pine-trees crusted with snow;
>
> And have been cold a long time
> To behold the junipers shagged with ice.[11]

Yet Wallace Stevens knew there is a "pressure of reality from without" as well as the poet's "pressure from within." He did not flinch from speaking of "earth feeling, sky that thinks." These notions gave him some philosophical pause, but they are the stuff of his poetry.

Our habit of mind is to reduce poetic language to something less than true. Instead, I hold poetic speech to be the original and pervasive form of truth, than which there is no higher. In Rosenstock-Huessy's missive from Heraclitus to Parmenides, the latter is represented as thinking that an expression such as "mother tongue" is a mere metaphor. Heraclitus replies: "For heaven's sake, Parmenides, 'mother tongue' is the original meaning of tongue." That is to say, the meaning of things is the way in which they present

---

[11] "The Snow Man" from *The Collected Poems of Wallace Stevens* (New York: Alfred A. Knopf, 1955), pp. 9–10.

themselves in their encounter with us. If, in the name of science and strict method, we change the terms of that encounter, we should at least be aware what we are doing.

To reach objective knowledge (so-called) one must *objectify*. Subjective knowledge, however (the only kind deserving of the name), does not require that we *subjectify*. Subjectivity is the natural condition of both knower and known. I am sure, dear Tillich, you agree with this, at least. So I will end my letter with a few remarks about theology and nature that I think can cause you no offense.

Everything I have said about verbs and nouns, about being and doing, about images, symbols and energy, about knowledge as intersubjective intercourse, implies that a human being's first and true business lies with nature. The attitudes I am espousing are those of natural religion and of its heirs in the modern world, which are poetry and the other arts. This is the womb out of which theology, like all other disciplines of thought, has come.

I read the history of Christian theology as a tragedy, of which Sophocles' *Oedipus Rex* may serve as a model. The conscious motive of Oedipus was to bring truth to light. The unconscious motive, the destiny prepared for him, was to return to his mother's womb. Between his conscious and his unconscious motive there stands a great taboo. Teiresias and Jocasta, who intuit the unconscious motive, say, "Look no further. You already know more than you can see." Oedipus, in touch only with the conscious motive, says, "I will ferret all things out." In the end, Oedipus is blind; yet, like Teiresias, he then sees more than do the eyes of reason and moral purpose.

To avoid incest and patricide, the Jewish and Christian religions fled from nature. They turned from the Earthly Mother to the Heavenly Father, from power *in* nature to power *over* nature, from the *many* to the *One*. The conscious motive was transcendence—God transcending the world, rational categories transcending experience.

Here is a motive no less noble than Oedipus', full of honor, principle, morality, and courage. Its high point in philosophy was Scholasticism; in religion, the stern transcendence of Calvinism. Then and there the rejected world, the unconscious motive, took over. In the seventeenth and eighteenth centuries, reason itself asked for and received a natural worship. In nineteenth-century Romanticism, feelings asserted their claim. In the twentieth century, demons arrived. We have the sense of living among uncontrollable forces that would as soon devour us as not. The natural world is the forbidden mother's womb, all dark, seething, and taboo to those for whom transcendence is God. We forget that through Jocasta's womb Oedipus, knowing it not, tunneled his way to the beatific grove at Colonus.

All verbs are pagan. The leaf stirs. The bird calls. Chronos stalks my pleasures. A natural spirit inhabits every verb. Either the world is animate or it is not.

If the world be not animate, no God can rule over it. Nothing can be ruled, loved, punished, saved, acted upon unless it can run, love, fight, flee, cry, laugh, respond. You cannot even breathe life *into* something unless it can inhale.

It seems then to me that if we destroy the pagan verbs by the alchemy of transmuting them into nouns, we bleed not only the pantheon but also any God who can traffic with the world.

God is not a theologian, and God can endure theology as literature endures its criticism. But theology cannot endure forever a fixation upon its own conscious motive. Even now it is being thrown back upon a culture alive with pagan force. It fears this as Oedipus feared his destiny. As the Greeks knew, however, a destiny cannot be avoided. It can only be made more costly by the attempt to run away.

As in tragedy, it is theology's *virtues* that are now heading toward ruin. As with Nicodemus, it is theology's *treasures* that are the price of salvation. By these virtues and treasures I mean theology's ability to *conceive* of God as Being Itself, as Wholly Other, as Telos of Hope, as First Cause, as Ultimate Horizon, and so on. By salvation I mean descent into the watery verbs, where nothing is but what it does and where the Spirit moves like a bird over sighs too deep for words. This mystery of verb that goes to chaos, and chaos that makes a verb, is that to which all literature testifies from its pagan heart. Let theology listen, for the Spirit will be pagan before it consents to die.

As you know, dear Tillich, your wife Hannah has written a book about the pagan relation she shared with you for all those years. Some found it denigrating, but I found it full of life gasping for life. I find that in your pages, too. If I quarrel, it is because I want to let Being stand aside and pay attention to the gasp.

Breathe well,

Tom

Letting Go

FEELING himself in danger of falling, the theologian sat down.

He had already fallen from grace at the place where he taught. "Down, down, down!" he had shouted at the president, voicing his dire prediction of the way things were going, after which he had himself gone down to despondency.

. He had no more control over the way the school was going than over the White House of Nixon, and in both cases history was taking him were he did not want to go. Never had he such a feeling of imminent collapse.

He got out of bed at dawn, brewed coffee, lit a cigarette, took pencil and paper, and sat down. Pencil and paper were instruments of exorcism.

He let feeling sponsor memory, and promptly the screen in the projection room of his mind was full. He let the film run, familiar as it was. When it was new it was called "The Theologian and the Big Beast"; now it seemed to have been reissued as "Wallowing in Watergate."

He was back in May 1973, in a meeting room at the

seminary where he taught. A group of faculty had assembled to approve a call to a famous scholar from across the sea. Nothing stood in the way of this action except the known reservations of two persons in the room, one of whom was the theologian himself. He believed the call was futile, that (as it later turned out) the appointee would not accept, and that the faculty's fascination with overseas scholars of fame deflected it from attending to candidates who, with lesser fame, had more pertinence to the theological agenda in America.

He had sat in the meeting pondering this. He guessed (rightly) that if he spoke he would change no votes. He guessed (wrongly) that his colleagues would like it if he expressed his mind anyway. Most knew where he stood, but only a few had heard his reasons. He rehearsed in his head how to make his points clear, brief, dispassionate. He did not want to stir up emotions when he had no hope of winning the vote.

Where his calculations went wrong, so it seemed to him now, was in his failure to divine the meaning of the lopsided vote he anticipated. A more political person would have realized that such a division reflected deeply held opinions on both sides of the house and stubborn interpretations of history. But the theologian, though he preached the power of gestalts and emotions, was in practice often a rationalist. He had the illusion that his reasons for his stance would commend themselves, if not to convert his opponents then and there, at least to inform their judgment on some subsequent occasion. At that moment, as in many others when he was participant rather than observer, it did not occur to him that one very frequent response to reason is vindictiveness. Nor did it occur to him that regarding oneself to be rational is very often the mask of one's own vindictiveness. He was saying to himself, "Be rational," forgetting that reason, like love, will seldom come by command, since it is the product of an open relation with the environment. Cognizant of all this in theory, and blind to its point at this moment, he misjudged himself. It followed that he misread the situation in the room. A truer sense was to arrive minutes later like a thunderclap.

Sweet reason opened the dialogue. The theologian gained the floor at a tactful time and bespoke himself for some ten minutes. He surveyed his interpretation of modern theology and the educational tasks of the Seminary. He reviewed the relation of American theology to European and spoke of the need to foster theological reflection upon the ethical issues that American life presents. He spoke of the authorities and sources theology uses to interpret the Christian gospel, and he emphasized awareness of specific, concrete experiences as one of those sources. He stressed the cultural component of theology, the better to say that the cultural transplantation of theologians, while it has worked brilliantly for some (Anselm, Tillich), is often a mistake. He argued (à la James Gustafson) that it was time American theology cut itself loose from overdependence on a "European theological matrix" the better to advance the contribution of America itself to "the theological tradition." So saying, he rested his case.

He was answered by his usual collegial antagonist. This man, who was his polar opposite in almost every respect, began in a mode of scholarly gentility. He thanked the speaker for having posed the issue in genuinely theological terms. He said that each of the points raised was of no little importance and that it well behooved our seminary to take them seriously. He declared that he hoped all our decisions would be made on the basis of such fundamental considerations. He took several minutes to turn over the theological propositions one by one, to show their significance, and to praise the theologian for having brought them forth.

Then the beast began to bite. The theologian, lulled by flattery, did not notice when the adversary's smile turned into a grimace. The first clue to reach him was the word *corruption*. He cocked his ear. The speaker was saying: ". . . unlike the old-fashioned kind of corruption we are used to. Today, we see something else: a corruption of the Constitution itself. So, too, Professor Driver's theology corrupts the theological tradition. We have here the theology of Watergate."

With that word the man stopped. In May, 1973, press and TV were then full of the cover-up that was coming apart one shred each day to reveal the shabby ruthlessness of the Nixon White House. It seemed to the theologian there was no more odious term to be used than *Watergate*. He was stunned.

Later a colleague reminded him that *odium theologicum* has an ancient history. It did not, however, belong to the style of their school, which instead affected an air of Victorian gentility. In fact, the whole scene being described was Victorian, or perhaps Edwardian like the architecture of the place. You could imagine the scene as an episode on stage: at the climactic moment, one well-dressed gentleman in a gathering has accused another of adultery. Such was the effect upon the theologian of the word Watergate.

Anger began to surge in him. Yet he was as afraid of his own anger as of the malice of the big beast, and most of all he feared losing face among his colleagues. He was in a state of paralyzing conflict. Later, one of his friends who was present said, "Why didn't you hit him?" Out of the question. Conflicted in every cell of his body, the theologian became catatonic. For some seconds he had no sensation whatever. Like a deer caught in the glare of headlights, he froze. His brain also shut down, no doubt to avoid too much awareness of rage.

What he looked like then, and how long the stun lasted, he would have given much to know. Slowly it came to him that he had to say something, for the room was completely still. If only he had had the grace to scream, or to cry, or to say, "Fuck you!" Any human, emotional response. But he had not the grace to utter his feeling. To do so was against the code of the room, and against all the Anglo-Saxonism in his heritage. He could not speak, nor move a muscle in his body, until he had found a formal way to do it.

Some seconds passed. To this day he still wondered how many. As if it made any difference. To the public, a brief instant, and of no matter anyhow. To him, the longest period in his adult life: the dark night when it became clear that he could not speak his mind without suffering for it.

He recalled many such times in childhood. The candid word rebuffed. The feeling of ostracism or shame for having said what was to him obvious. For instance, the day his parents had taken him for his first look at the ocean. He and his mother stood above the beach watching and hearing the surf. "Isn't it wonderful?" she had said. And he, no more than eight or nine, had, upon looking at the mighty water, been put in mind of the majesty of God, so that he saw this awesome phenomenon as, at most, the flick of God's finger. "What's so wonderful about it?" said he. She was offended, and gave him a look of silent, terrible reprobation. By such profound unwit he had got himself unjustified, outraged, frustrated; and now he was at the same point again, only this time as an adult. If you say what you mean, and if what you mean is not what is wanted, you will pay the price of ostracism. To be called Watergate was to be put beyond the moral pale.

He looked at the big beast in silence. He waited until a formal reply came to him. Then he said: "I hope, sir, that you are not suggesting that there is an analogy between my theology and Watergate."

The reply was quick: "Yes, that's exactly what I'm saying."

Brief pause. One more chance to respond with feeling. Opportunity refused. The theologian said, in a tone befitting the melodrama in which he fancied himself to be cast: "Then I request an apology."

The reply came: "Well, you won't get it!"

The room was silent with embarrassment. The theologian looked around. He was like one whose honor had been defamed near the second-act curtain, who knew that a duel should follow and wondered who would be his second. There were no volunteers. In the studied silence not a hair moved. The theologian glared, then waited, then sulked.

More time ticked by. Then the chairman intervened by changing the subject.

The theologian heard the meeting out, took note of the anticipated ballot, and went home to sound off about the indignity he had suffered.

The episode kept recurring in his memory as that of an intersection between public and private. That he had handled it badly he was well aware, for it was one of those public (or semipublic) occasions when he needed his anger and found himself suppressing it. This made for frustration, so he lived and relived the incident, as if by rehearsing it often enough in imagination he could make it come out right. Even a year later, after he first wrote a description of the scene, he had a dream in which, like Medusa, he had turned his big beast to stone simply by looking at him.

But what if he had handled the occasion well? Would that have made much difference? Probably not, for it is megalomania to think that if I do what is right all else will be well. The theologian had learned from Reinhold Niebuhr that a personal virtue is not sufficient answer to a social ill, whatever Billy Graham may say. When Graham says, "There is a little bit of Watergate in all of us," it is beside the point. Watergate falls like rain upon the just and the unjust. What we need to know is the state of the weather, what protection we need, and what resources we have for coping.

The fairest weather the theologian had known was during the storms of 1968. That was the time he had been in step with what he took to be history. The next three or four years were full of growth. The changes he experienced in himself were good and seemed to belong to the pace of the times. Yet by 1972 something had begun to go wrong. On the national scene, it was the Nixon reelection, an event that appeared ever more wrong the more one learned about it. Closer to home, 1972 was the year in which the movement for curricular reform in his own school peaked without accomplishing much, after which a conservative reaction set in. As for himself, 1972 was the year he realized he no longer had the strength of his youth. His son beat him at arm-wrestling. The theologian was forty-seven years old.

In the spring of 1968, when student rebellion broke out in Paris, he was on leave in Cambridge, England, an ideal place from which to observe the event at a distance. Soon Columbia University was in riot. This could not but affect his own school, which was right across the street and had close ties to the university. He received a long epistle about it from the president, a kindred spirit. They were both eager that the crisis, which neither of them would have fomented, should result in a stronger social conscience in the school. The theologian went every day to the reading room at King's College to follow the stories in the papers. Lyndon Johnson had announced his retirement that spring, his Vietnam policy discredited largely by student action. The murder of Martin Luther King, Jr., had shown that conservative America felt itself seriously threatened. (The FBI's harrassment of King was not yet known.) The students realized it was time to press hard. They chose to attack in the universities, where they had the greatest leverage.

The theologian did not share the students' rhetoric nor

their utopianism. He was a reformer, not a revolutionary. Still, he had been a teacher long enough to know that students are exploited by their schools. He sensed that schools are power structures, responsive in subtle as well as obvious ways to the political and economic entrenchments of society, more responsive to these (over the long run) than to truth for its own sake or to the impartial education of students. He believed that judgments about what is true, good, and beautiful are inevitably affected by self-interest and the way it functions in the political dimensions of a human situation, be it in the family, the school, the academic society, a profession, a business, or a government. He therefore felt that the politics of a school and its educational performance were closely connected. The aim was to see to it that no power within the school (or over it) could be exercised without the restraint of those whom that power affected. The trick was how to do this without turning the school into a populist democracy that would soon be led by demogogues.

When he went to Paris in early June of 1968, he found the streets at the Sorbonne full of uniformed police, almost the only people visible in that by-now subdued place. He had never before seen a university under siege, and he realized sadly what is the fate of a temple of truth that cannot justly govern itself. But he felt the lesson worth learning, and he knew clearly where his sympathies lay.

He returned to New York to find his own school at work on a plan of governance. Deeply torn by the Columbia riots, the school now pulled together in a remarkable way. It wrote a "Transitional Plan of Governance" that brought students and staff employees into the making of decisions at almost every level. A few students and a few faculty like the theologian thought its distribution of power did not go far enough, because it assured a faculty majority in the governing assembly and thus enabled the faculty, if it cared to vote *en bloc*, to hold sway without accountability; but it was pointed out that issues at the seminary rarely split along faculty-student lines, and in the prevailing mood of unity the school moved boldly into its future.

Or so it seemed. In the following March, the faculty was embattled over its presidency. In this fracas the theologian was roundly defeated. His candidate, having been elected by the board's search committee, was invited to the school for final discussions only to find himself the unhappy victim of a palace revolution. Certain faculty, including the theologian's big beast, threw tantrums and succeeded in getting the board to back down. The nominee was sent home empty-handed. The theologian and most other members were thrown off the search committee, which was reconstituted, and in due course a new candidate was chosen. (Four years later, the same throwers of tantrums sent *him* away empty-handed.)

The theologian did not well know how to interpret these events. He did not realize he was dealing with people who identified theology with academic conservatism, who therefore believed passionately that any attempt to revise educational method was theologically subversive. He did perceive that faculty, for the most part, resist any making of policy that threatens to impinge on their individuality, which they call "academic freedom"; but he thought this attitude a luxury that would surely pass as it became clear that the economy would not support schools merely for the sake of the scholarly independence of professors. He did not yet imagine what it would be like as the sixties became the seventies, when a mood of conservatism would settle over the whole country, all schools would be retrenching, and as their economic situation became steadily worse the more would they turn again to modes of education centered upon the prerogatives and expertise of the individual teacher. Not forseeing this, the theologian went his own way and exercised his individuality after his fashion.

In April of 1969 he found himself at the Esalen Institute in California. He went there to scoff and found himself, in accordance with the dire predictions of his enemies, caught up in the so-called Human Potential Movement. He came to believe in the enthusiasm of the counterculture, latched on to Paul Goodman as a *philosophe,* and took to the cultural analyses of Theodore Roszak.

To the joy of some and the dismay of others, his Esalen ventures began to transform his teaching in 1970. Asked for the first time to offer the main introductory course in theology, he devised a way to run it like an experiential workshop, the aim being to bring to consciousness the connections, usually hidden, between experiences and theological opinions.

He recalled the day he had gone into the Comptroller's office to request that the room he would use for this course be stripped of all furniture and supplied with a carpet. The Comptroller had eyed him at length and then said, "Driver, you are starting an educational revolution here; and we are not set up to handle it." The theologian returned the look and gently replied, "That's right. But, you know, it's only a *small* revolution, and we could *get* set up to handle it." The Comptroller did not move his eyes while he reached for the phone and asked for his assistant. He spoke to the mouthpiece: "Driver wants 205 with no chairs and a rug on the floor." Pause. "How the hell do I know what he wants to do in there?"

The success of the course blinded the theologian to much that was going on in other quarters. He was deluded also by the machinery the school set in motion to reform itself. During 1971–72, the new president set up a duly elected Planning Group to formulate long-range policy. The theologian served as Chairperson of a task force that proposed to bring Black students and faculty to number one-third of the total at the school and women, one-half. To his surprise, this proposal, which later was said to have got the school into all kinds of trouble, was adopted all the way up the line with a minimum of controversy. By the end of the spring term in 1972, when the theologian went on leave, the Planning Group report was adopted. It called for three major policies to be implemented: the recruitment of Blacks and women, the redesign of the Master of Divinity Degree in a more "professional" direction (that is, more closely related to the exercise of ministry in local communities), and the development of interdisciplinary projects among the faculty in what was called a "collegial style." The following year, the theologian, although he was on leave, acceded to the president's request to work on the professional degree design team. Efforts to implement the other two recommendations got almost nowhere, though the number of women students did increase of its own accord.

On the whole, the momentum for educational change, which had peaked in 1968–69, ran out in 1972–73. Officially, it was still going. But every move on the surface, procedural or substantive, felt instantly the drag of a powerful undertow. It was like rowing a boat against a current you could feel but not see, meanwhile being urged to row harder and being cheered from the side by the president, the development office, and all manner of friends in faraway places. The rhythm of the rowing team became ragged. The design team's report was a tapestry of compromise.

In 1973–74 the undercurrent surfaced. The governing assembly (which by the end of the year had voted itself out of existence), the faculty, and finally the administration, spent the year in a series of decisions as if in systematic repeal of 1968. The theologian had never before been among a group of people so busily and avidly engaged in undoing their own previous commitments, and while this was accomplished at the cost of much anguish on the part of many, it was clearly the desire of most. The year ended with the resignation of the president, repudiated by the very people who had sought him out and hired him.

The theologian was despondent. He did not mind adversity. He did not even mind losing battles. What he did mind was alienation. He did not like having to guess what people were thinking. He did not like situations that he could read but not fathom. Nor did it help much when observers he trusted told him that the school was simply "out of touch," for he disliked all out-of-touchness, having quite enough of his own. He desired to be among people more aware than himself, but now he had too few of them. He was on his own, and he was frightened. He masked the fear beneath despondency, sleeping little and never coming quite awake.

If only things looked better when he turned to wider horizons. In this summer of impeachment, or near-impeachment (who knew which?), it seemed as if the whole land was masking its fear with quietude. The nation was adrift. A friend of his tried to phone a government agency in Washington and got no answer. "Maybe," she put it to the long-distance operator, "the whole government is shut down." "I wouldn't be surprised," came the reply.

Contemporary history, the kind you see in the news every day, had become one of those situations the theologian could read but not fathom. This was new in his life. He had been used to living through epochs of rather clear dramatic and ethical character. His earliest memories of the public world were of the depression and the New Deal, a period the critic Harold Clurman later aptly called "the fervent years." They were followed by war. The theologian finished high school and went off to the army—fully if not happily resigned to defending "the free world." Home un-scathed, he had gone to college during the melodrama of McCarthyism and Cold War. This sequence put him in seminary, graduate school, and first teaching during the Eisenhower years, which were certainly not fervent, but the theologian then had his own agenda so full he did not share the nation's lassitude, though he noticed it. He had married, pursued a Ph.D., fathered two children, adopted another, lucked into a good job, and worked around the clock to establish a reputation for himself. He knew well enough that Eisenhower represented a dangerous complacency in the American character, but he was too busy getting ahead to do much about it. So he was a complicitor. The sixties rescued him, either from the complicity or from the appearance of it. He was exhilarated by the New Frontier. Kennedy liberalism, which in retrospect seemed a bit phony, was at the time made for the likes of him. He deeply wanted to "get the country moving again," and he shared the sense of hope that ran then through the nation. He wrote a piece on the occasion of T. S. Eliot's death in 1965 saying sadly that the poet did not share the hope of the present generation. It did not occur to the theologian to write a theology of hope, and had he done so it would have been different from Jurgen Moltmann's; but he understood the motives and applauded them.

After Kennedy was shot, there were two escalations: the war in Vietnam and Black liberation at home. Both were part of an even larger change that had occurred, imperceptibly at first, about 1960. Until then, throughout the theologian's life, it had been possible for an educated person to view world history as if its essence were European. When the theologian was in college, a buddy pointed out to him one day that all their courses started with Aristotle. That did seem odd, but he was not able then to grasp the import of it. When he joined the civil rights movement during its embryonic stage in the late forties—when Bayard Rustin and others started integrating interstate buses in the South—he did not imagine that racial equality in America would, if ever it came, mark the end of the European cultural hegemony. Why should he think so? There was little or no revisionist history in those days. Was not Europe the haven for Black writers (Negroes at the time) who wanted to escape the racial stereotypes they faced in America? Wasn't Europe the fountainhead of those very liberties inscribed in the American Constitution, to which Negro citizens were now claiming entitlement? Wasn't the civil rights movement part of the fulfillment of the American dream, and wasn't that dream the New World culmination of the democratic ideal from Athens onward? Finally, was it not a matter of Providence that Europe was the carrier of Christianity, the necessary source of the moral fervor required of free people? Such, in 1948, was the young theologian's amalgam of Christianity, the Enlightenment, Hegel, and Babbitt.

He was shaken out of this shallow eclecticism in seminary, by Reinhold Niebuhr, Karl Barth, Paul Tillich, and James Muilenberg, his Old Testament professor. Yet even they, who taught him to distinguish Christianity from culture and who knocked his naive progressivism out of him, did nothing to disabuse his notion that Christianity lives under the authority of a "tradition" inseparable from the history of Europe. On the contrary, they reinforced this view.

Reflecting on himself in 1974, the theologian realized that he had indeed changed. He remembered his colleague John Bennett's opener when they had run into each other in the crowded lobby of the Century Plaza Hotel at a conference in Los Angeles in 1972: "My, you have changed!"

"Do I look so different?"

"No, I don't mean that. You used to be a classicist."

"What makes you think I'm not now?"

"They say you've changed."

Something in him had broken with something that was there before, no doubt was still there yet without the same authority. He did not agree that he was no longer a classicist, though surely he had ceased to be what some other people though a classicist was. Moreover, this change had much to do with the big beast's allegation about Watergate. He wanted to see this more clearly.

His mind kept hovering over the spring of 1964. There was something 'round about that time to be sniffed out.

He could hear James Baldwin's voice and see the look in his eyes as they sat together on the couch in Baldwin's apartment on West End Avenue with Sidney Lanier and a number of others busy in the room. With a twinkle and a shrug Baldwin had said, "Your days are numbered."

In those numbered days, the theologian was a drama critic as well as a seminary teacher. In 1962 he had gone off to France for a year, and while there had begun to write a history of the modern theater. When he came back in the fall of 1963, he did not resume his theater pieces for *The Christian Century* but instead became the critic for *The Reporter*, then the most widely read of the liberal magazines. Its founder, publisher, and editor was Max Ascoli, once a refugee from Mussolini's Italy, who had achieved fame for himself and his journal by launching it with fearless denunciations of Senator Joseph McCarthy. The managing editor now was Robert Bingham, who had sought out the theologian by letter in Europe and taken him on as drama critic.

In April of 1964, Broadway had a play by James Baldwin, *Blues for Mister Charlie*. In those days a drama on Broadway by a Black author was a rarity. The most recent of note had been *Raisin in the Sun*, by Lorraine Hansbury, which the theologian/critic had been almost alone in finding superficial. He remembered how pained he had been to find himself putting down Hansbury's play, which Kenneth Tynan, writing for *The New Yorker*, had said was "on the side of life."

Baldwin was not a dramatist, but he was an author of great rhetorical power, and *Blues for Mr. Charlie* was a play that required attention. By and large, the reviewers hated it. They tore its style, dialogue, characterization, and structure to pieces. They said it was blatant propaganda and no good kind of play at all. It was as if Baldwin, who had recently written *The Fire Next Time*, had now got hold of a piece of kindling, put a match to it right there on Broadway, and all the critics were out with fire-hoses. Their nozzles sputtered, sprayed, and squirted. The play got wet and started to die.

The theologian/critic thought the other critics had either missed the point or were determined to refuse it. He went to his typewriter. The play had moved him very much for two main reasons, not counting the fine performances of Diana Sands and Pat Hingle. First, the authenticity of the characters and their attitudes had sat him bolt upright in his seat. He, a Southerner, had seldom seen on stage or film a representation of Southern folk that was half as close to his own memoried images. Only Tennessee Williams came to his mind to compare. Even so, Williams wrapped his characters in myth, which made it possible to hold them at a certain distance, while Baldwin purported to "tell it like it is." The theologian/critic from Tennessee was sure that Baldwin's eyes and ears had not failed him.

Second, the play was angry. They were right who said it was propaganda. If they wanted their propaganda subtle, they would not get it from the author of *The Fire Next Time*. And the theologian/critic sensed something else about the anger. It was not only Baldwin's. It bespoke an anger in the Black soul, and it was a harbinger of things to come. The theologian heard in the play the roll of distant thunder. He saw flashes of lightning. At that time, the civil rights movement was led by a nonviolent hero, Martin Luther King, Jr. Watts had not yet burned, nor Detroit, Newark, and Harlem. Cleaver and Newton were not heard from, nor Soledad nor Angela Davis. Whites were not conscious of Black Panthers, and most did not know of Malcolm X. There was no such thing, known to white people at least, as Black Theology. The theologian/critic could only guess about the storm to come, but one thing seemed unmistakable in the play: Black people saw and sympathized with the plight of White liberals, and they were prepared nonetheless to walk straight over them. If this were the case, if such an attitude came to prevail among Black people, a new and unpredictable force would enter upon the American scene.

The play arrived on the eve of Black Power. That phrase was introduced by Stokely Carmichael the following summer. Meanwhile it was spring, Robert Moses's New York World's Fair was going on, and the biggest rumble was a threat by the Brooklyn chapter of CORE to tie up traffic on the Triborough Bridge.

The theologian/critic wrote his piece about *Blues for Mr.*

Charlie and sent it off routinely to the magazine. He acknowledged that the play had flaws, but he insisted its depictions were only too true, that it held its largely Black audience enthralled (in those days not many Black people went to Broadway), and that as a social document it was more important than anything else in recent theater. Along the way, the theologian/critic managed to say that the racial conflict ahead of us could not be avoided or well addressed by "doctrinaire liberalism."

The telephone rang. It was Bob Bingham to say that they were not going to print the review of *Blues for Mr. Charlie*.

Why the hell not? The answer was vague; the critic pressed the question. Finally Bingham replied: "Well, when you said what you did about doctrinaire liberalism you stepped on our toes."

"Good God!" the critic blurted, "I didn't know anybody *confessed* to being a doctrinaire liberal."

"Well," said Bingham, "I guess they do."

"Let me think this over," said the critic. "I'll talk to you later."

While he was thinking, the phone rang again. It was Sidney Lanier, rector of St. Clement's Episcopal Church and cofounder of the American Place Theater. Had the theologian/critic seen *Blues for Mr. Charlie*? What did he think of it? Why wasn't his review out yet? The theologian/critic explained. Lanier: "Oh. Well, look. Some of us are down here at Baldwin's place trying to figure out how to save the play. Why don't you come on down?"

So he went, and sat on the couch, and told Baldwin what had happened with *The Reporter*. And Baldwin's eyes twinkled, and he shrugged and said, "Your days are numbered."

When the theologian left there, he called Bingham. "I've thought it over. I'll take out the offensive language about liberalism."

"I don't know," said Bingham. "Ascoli is very angry. I don't know what he'll say."

"Let me talk to him."

"He's too angry. He won't talk to you. I'll call you back. It may be tomorrow. I hope he cools off."

Bingham called back the next day. "The answer is no."

"No, what?"

"No, we won't run the review, no matter if you change it."

Pause. "Let me get this straight. Are you telling me that the drama critic for *The Reporter* magazine may not say what he wants to say about this play no matter how he says it?"

"I guess I am."

"You don't have a drama critic."

Word that *The Reporter* had attempted to censor, and had therefore lost, its drama critic got around, even into the newspapers. There was some tit for tat about whether the critic had quit or was fired. *The Reporter* started getting letters of protest and subscription cancellations. It prepared a form letter to answer them. One of these was sent to Eric Bentley, dean of American drama critics, who went up in smoke at receiving a form letter in response to his personal note to Ascoli. The principal liberal journal in the country

had, in the Baldwin play, come up against an issue it refused
to cope with. Happily, the critic had not known that Ascoli
was already mad at Baldwin because of *The Fire Next Time*.
Ascoli was one of the first editors to publish Baldwin, years
before, and he felt betrayed by the author's anger.

The quashed review was immediately printed by *Christianity and Crisis* and *The Village Voice*, and thereafter by
Black Digest, becoming the most-printed review the theologian had written during his nine years as a critic. He received
a message from his old paper, *The Christian Century*. It said,
"This would never have happened to you here. Come
home." The theologian decided instead to finish his history
of the modern theater, and he spent the rest of the sixties
doing it.

The writing of that book in that decade had a lasting effect
on the theologian. He remembered his colleague, Wilhelm
Pauck, telling him not to do it. Pauck had strong opinions
about everything, usually negative. The theologian told
him one evening that he'd gotten a contract to write a history of the modern theater and had started work on it.
Pauck said it was a mistake. He seemed to think the theologian should write a book of theology instead. However, it
was the theologian's nature always to do theology while
appearing to do something else, so he paid no attention.

As it turned out, the modern theater book did not have
much theology in it; but it had lots of reflections on modern
culture, and these helped the theologian to get a perspective
on the theology he used most, which was Paul Tillich's. He

made now a list of what he had come to think while writing the book—opinions and ideas that represented the way he had "changed."

1. That "modern" culture is over. Along about 1960 it changed into something different, which he called "contemporary."
2. That "modern" culture had gone a bit mad in its obsession with historical thinking. This gave rise to the "antihistorical bias" so many teachers complained of in their students.
3. That the European tradition was no longer normative. It had been "used up" by writers like Joyce and Beckett, so worked over by historians that all they could do now was to footnote it. Besides, it got in the way of our recognition of the "Third World" at home and abroad.
4. The correlation Paul Tillich made between theology and culture would, as Tillich predicted, have to be redrawn, since the culture had changed. (Only later did the theologian come to think that the "method of correlation" itself, along with its ontological starting point, had to be challenged.)
5. Both the Church and the theater, as we mostly know them, are so tied to the European tradition that they get lost when its authority wanes. Our churches are imagined to be medieval parishes, adapting to modernity as best they can a theological and liturgical tradition evolved in the vicissitudes of Europe. Our theaters are Baroque opera houses, holding on to an esthetic of *mimesis* derived long ago from the Greeks. The alienation that the church and the theater both feel from contempo-

rary culture cuts across the distinction between "sacred" and "secular," which is not very helpful anyway.

One night in 1966 the theologian was invited to a symposium at St. Mark's Place, an off-Broadway theater. Peter Brook's production of the *Marat/Sade* was current, had attracted much attention, and Brook was to participate with Leslie Fiedler, Ian Richardson the actor, and some others in a conference starting at midnight so that theater people could attend after their evening shows. The caucus turned into a pow-wow about the theater in our culture. It was a very "in" discussion. Almost everyone there lived for the theater. In the wee morning hours they let down their hair and lamented the plight of their art. The theater was losing its audience. Not for almost twenty years had the theater been really *important*, neither to the average person nor to the taste-makers. Lionel Trilling, for instance, had recently introduced a collection of Ingmar Bergman's screenplays by saying that nowadays he went more often to movies than to plays, no longer considering theater essential to his knowledge of culture. The theologian was beginning to feel the same way, he who for years had been explaining to all and sundry how the theater was an art far superior to film. Everyone saw that theater had moved to the edge of things. They mourned over this like the sad keepers of some holy flame. The theater was *good*, and it was good for *people*, and it communicated a certain order of truth not to be gotten in any other way, and the people had gone away from it and would not come back. How could we get them back? Or take the theater to them, wherever they were? Surely Peter

Brook, the directorial genius and pundit, knew the answer. But he did not. At four A.M. everyone went sadly away.

At three the next afternoon the theologian sat in seminary faculty meeting. The faculty were asking what should be done about daily chapel services. The services were very good. They were essential to the Christian life, and especially to a seminary. Some of the most important ideas in the history of the place had been enunciated in chapel in the old days, even within the living memory of those present. What was a seminary without regular corporate worship? There is no substitute for liturgy. But the people had gone away and would not come back. (The theologian thought of Sam Goldwyn: "If the people don't want to come, nothing can stop them.") Public worship, in the seminary as in the church, had moved to the edge of things. Even a great number of the faculty were not to be seen in chapel. Apparently they no longer considered it essential. Surely the president, or that faculty member who wrote books and taught courses on worship, knew what to do about it. But they did not. Daily chapel was discontinued.

The theologian was fascinated by the near identity of the two discussions. The script for one was the scenario for the other. The theater people did not talk about religion, and the seminary faculty did not talk about theater; but their experiences were alike and their responses the same. He thought, as for other reasons he had often thought before, that theater and church are twins. They often fight, but they come in tandem from the same womb, and their fates are intertwined. Now the theologian found himself partially alienated from both, although it was to both of them that he

had devoted his career. There was some need, created in
contemporary experience, that could not be met on a regular basis by the forms we know as church and theater. Occasionally, yes. Let a catastrophe occur (like the assassination
of John Kennedy) and the churches are full next Sunday.
They swell also at Christmas and Easter. So, too, in the
theater there are a few hits, and a certain public goes to see
the curtain rise once in a while. But the theologian/critic
knew that the social meaning of an art is to be judged by its
regular, not its spectacular, function. The theater had long
been a fabulous invalid, and the church had become a holy
cripple. Nothing new in *that* and nothing wrong with it
from the point of view of esthetics or theology, neither of
which should use sheer popularity as a criterion of value.
What did matter was the defection of so many of the faith-
ful and, worse, the dispirited tone of those who remained.
In other words, the theater and the church were losing, or
had lost, their power as public symbols.

In the seminaries, the response to this ill fate of the church
was remarkable. Theologians tended to be scornful of the
very profession they were training people for. In fact, they
didn't train them for it if they could help it. They turned
them into teachers. That was how the theologian himself
had come to be where he was. He had entered seminary
intending (at least he thought he intended) to take a degree
and go back down South to be a preacher where he belonged. The president of the school had told him, however,
that he surely didn't want to waste his life that way. He
promptly changed plans and took a job at that same seminary as soon as it was offered.

The tendency (not in theory but in practice) to look down upon the church and its ministry was so strong in the theologian that he could spot it quickly in others. And there was plenty of public evidence, the clearest being that the so-called practical field in the curriculum had nothing like the prestige of the "classical disciplines." Every move to make the latter more responsive to the former met with defeat. Meanwhile, the attempt to conform church practice to seminary theory was equally fruitless. Once, one of the deans told him flatly that the churches were going to become empty, just as they already were in England, and the only place to maintain "the tradition" would be in the university. The theologian had no evidence to show that the churches would *not* become empty, but the statement helped him to clarify his own bias. He was not going to end up maintaining a "tradition" in the refugee camp of a university. His interest in theology had never been arcane, and he would give it up before he became its curator.

The birds were singing at midday. The sun gave off a July heat through still air. The theologian went to get a cool drink as the lines of his Watergate came into focus around him.

He had had a good education—in high school as well as college, seminary, and graduate English. In the sixties this good education began to fail him. He became aware of it gradually. Little by little he saw that he was culturebound. He had grown up in the Appalachians. He had gone to Europe with the army, to college in North Carolina, and thereafter to New York. Until he was thirty-seven years

old, he had never crossed the American continent, although
by then he had been to Europe five times. He had studied no
non-European language. He had not the slightest interest in
going to Latin America. He believed that the religions of
Asia were for the Asians. Their worst error, he had been
taught, was their failure to "take history seriously," which
had been the crowning achievement of biblical and European thought. True product of his education, he was almost
obsessed with historical consciousness. He wrote his doc-
toral dissertation on the sense of history in Shakespeare and
the Greeks. His book on the modern theater showed the
theater's reflection of historical consciousness since the
French Revolution. He was proud of both these books yet
realized he was no longer preoccupied with their themes.
His education belonged to the epoch of World War II, its
prelude, duration, and aftermath. And what was World War
II? He understood it to be the defense of European-
American civilization against barbarism.

If at any time you had called the young theologian a racist,
he would have been outraged. Had he not been liberated
from that by the careful nurture of the director of Christian
education in the Methodist church where he grew up? Had
he been called a Nigger-lover in the army for nothing? Who
was in the civil rights movement much earlier than he? And
so on. Very slowly did he come to see that racism is not only
a moral (that is, an immoral) attitude but, even more deeply,
a *cultural* attitude, that one who cannot stand outside one's
own culture and know it to be parochial must have the
dispositions of a racist. If you grow up in a minority, you
will almost surely see the parochialism of culture, because

you will experience the ways in which (Sam Goldwyn again) it includes you out; but if you grow up in a majority, this is hard to see, and harder still to *feel*.

The attack upon racism in America in the early sixties posed a threat to the normative value of the European cultural tradition. The attack could not have made such headway as it did if the wars in Korea and Vietnam, the revolution in Cuba, revolutionary movements in South America, strife in the Middle East, the independence of African states, Maoism in China, wealth in Japan, and floods of international literature, film and TV had not required that a third world had to be seen in addition to those familiar two that faced each other across barbed wire in Europe.

The position of the United States in the new picture was ambiguous. On the one hand, the U. S. was the inheritor of the European tradition, the ally of Europe, and the new wielder of Europe's imperial power. The war in Vietnam showed this, for the U. S. took over that war in receivership from the French. On the other hand, the United States had subcultures that never belonged to the European tradition, and many persons and groups who had belonged were defecting. Popular music of the fifties and sixties was changed worldwide by infusion of modalities from Black America with a good deal of country corn thrown in. Rock was taken up by the counterculture and exploited for its subversive potential. Then Rock was co-opted by big business. That was the nature of America: it built subversion into itself, forestalling all political and socioeconomic revolution, chewing up its own cultural values (whether conservative or revolutionary), strip mining its own moral landscape, changing itself into something neither old nor new, neither East nor West, a monster for which all things are possible.

The theologian was very ambivalent about America. He was, however, sure that it presented to the intellect and to theology a challenge which "the European tradition" could not meet. The churches were finding this out, for their existence bore almost no relation to the preoccupations of theology, except for the very conservative churches and their fanatical theology, which were booming. Here was the Hellenistic Age all over again: a massive power of empire thrown over a culture that had long since lost its integrity, the people spiritually hungry (not to say starving), religious cults everywhere, the "official" religion powerless except in fanatical form, the arts reduced to consumer goods.

The theologian was designated, in 1973, Professor of Theology and Culture just at the time when he came to believe that the culture was in shambles.

A white moth flew lazily in the air. Of what was the theologian the custodian? Little or nothing, and did not want to be. It was an attitude you might regard as a cop-out or, as he saw it, the condition of responsiveness. To what? To God, he thought.

The day got stiller. He pondered the arrogance of what he was thinking. Who was he to know the condition of responsiveness to God? And to say that he had it? He waited to see if the earth would swallow him up.

Go on with it. Don't stop now. The big beast thinks you are demonic. Own up before the lines once more go out of focus.

The split ran throughout the culture and was very apparent in education. Every school he knew was divided between "traditionalists" and whatever the others were called. In his own school the phrase that stuck, coined by one of his antagonists, was "classicists vs. romantics." The theologian was irritated by this cliché, but there it was. In theological education the split was fierce because (in the nondenominational schools, at least) money was getting scarce. People were being let go. Everyone was edgy.

In such a situation, and with the culture in shambles, was it not cavalier to refuse to be custodial? Did not one have to maintain the school in any case, and what was the school for if not to preserve a tradition of learning—the library, the history of theological ideas, the study of Scripture, the bearing of these upon the present and the future? Such is the task of education, *a fortiori* of theological education, since it belongs to a tradition defined by continuity with the revelation once given in Jesus the Christ.

He was not *against* any of this. Quite the opposite. He was only against its coming to be the definition of what mattered. The trouble was that the argument usually shaped up as "tradition" vs. "change." Of course, the traditionalists were not against all change, since they knew perfectly well that a static tradition is a dying tradition. Its days are numbered. But the issues were always put in terms of how much change vs. how much tradition. You preserved the tradition by changing it, always changing the least amount possible in order to do the minimum damage to the tradition.

It was as if there were two values, one to be called tradition (or memory), the other called change (or anticipation). Traditionalists were brokers who stood in the middle, mak-

ing sure that the adjustments between the two were fair.
Since memory is short and change inevitable, they were
usually to be found arguing the case of tradition.

The theologian thought there must be a third way. He
was tired of the same arguments over and over, no matter
what the topic.

The birds kept on singing, and then he remembered a
time when he had fallen into a third way. If he had changed,
and if one wanted a moment to mark it, that one would
serve, for there was no moment more vivid in his resignation from custodianship.

They were standing around, wondering what to do. The
most distraught was Betty Fuller, the leader of this
"couples' workshop," whose intuition rarely failed her.
The theologian was the center of their attention. They had
been working with him nearly an hour. The point of his
sticking was clear to everybody, including him: he would
give everything except himself, and this ultimate reserve
had brought his communication with his wife to a standstill.
He was carefully measuring how much tradition and how
much change he would admit in their relation.

To do that, of course, he had to maintain his own version of the tradition. The way *he* remembered events in
their marriage was the way they *were*. The things *he* remembered were the important things, and those he forgot
had no significance. He was the official historian of the marriage, because he was the custodian of its values.

Truth to tell, her memory was more ample than his, and
he was aware of that. Dates, names, places, who was there,
who wasn't, ages of people's children, sometimes including

his own—all these things she could usually come up with when they slipped his mind. Good. She was an excellent archivist. Entirely fitting that her profession should be that of a medieval historian, the age of chroniclers and scribblers. But (ultimate put-down) she could not be trusted to see the tradition aright. Any tradition. Neither that of medieval theology, which she read constantly, nor that of their marriage. When push came to shove, he shoved; the marriage was in his custody and he had to protect it, from God knows what. His name for this was "faithfulness."

Since they were devoted to each other and had no thought of splitting, he could not understand why she did not share his sense of protecting the marriage. She seemed to take their relation for granted, a most dangerous attitude. And what he called protection she called possessiveness. She was blithe, except when friction occurred; then she became stubborn as a mule. She seemed to want nothing from the marriage except to get on with it and live it. This, he was perfectly sure, was because she came from Florida. They had no mountains there, no rocks, no trees hundreds of years old. They were southern but not Southerners. They lived on shallow, sandy soil, and they grew up basking in the sun. She could not understand the long history of value he brought to the marriage, and unless he remained conscious of this the whole arrangement would go awry.

To keep hold on himself was all the more important at Esalen. California was almost as rootless as Florida. They were, at the time, in San Francisco, which he loved, but where had Esalen chosen to hold this workshop? In some nondescript basement room in a Unitarian Church! He was out of place, and so was another member of the group, a distinguished-looking Presbyterian elder some sixty-five years of age who had obviously come there only to please his wife, a woman who also appeared not to understand the protective virtues of her husband, a kindly man, though perhaps a bit stiff. And what is wrong with stiffness? No tradition without backbone. Esalen, California, Florida, Hawaii, Unitarianism—the domains of jellyfish.

The workshop was stalled right now. Betty Fuller had become suspicious of the theologian's ability, where his wife was concerned, to see only what he saw and hear only what he heard. She didn't trust his memory. She suggested that they reenact the scene of their most recent spat. Theologian and wife both remembered it well, so they said. "Fine," said Betty. "Then swap roles. You play her, and she'll play you."

Marvelous. He was a born actor and a theater critic. These workshops are fun. Besides, here's a good chance to show how wife brings about these spats. I'll get some help.

His wife was shy about doing the scene. She had never liked acting, didn't think it was her bag, was so little an exhibitionist that even this closed room was too big a stage for her. But she was willing, and they began.

He blew it. Knew instantly when he had done so. Saw it coming, and felt powerless to stop it. In her role, he lost his temper, lashed out in a torrent of invective. Oops! Bad show. That's not what she does. It's what *he* does. What does *she* do? No idea. Can't think. No memory. She must do something, and it must be terrible because the script is supposed to get dreadful along about here. But he had no idea. He blew it. Then he lied. That is, he bluffed. Maybe they won't have noticed. Maybe she *does* lose her temper and I'll have played it right after all. He kept going. No use. The scene was out of focus and everybody knew it. He got the message from the way she looked at him. They stopped, and the workshop stalled.

She told him later that attempting his role had been one of the hardest things she'd ever tried. He had many occasions thereafter to observe that most couples find role-swapping very difficult. But even if he had known these things at the time it would not have mattered, because he had himself to deal with. It was clear that he was standing in his own way. He would not give himself up. He had himself in custody. As he treated himself he treated others, too. The price he paid for his mechanism of control was the loss of spontaneous feeling. It put him out of touch. It gave him a sense of danger, which called for ever more control.

As awareness of this syndrome began to present itself right there in the room, he began to fidget. He wanted out of his pattern. He had no rehearsal, no experience, of how to get out; so he became ruthless, like an animal in a cage. The group turned its attention to him. He felt like an animal at bay. They had found his lair. He was full of energy and had no place to go. It was not the group that trapped him. He knew that. The group, just by looking at him, was a mirror in which he could see himself pushing at the walls of an invisible cage. He had himself at bay. The workshop stalled.

"What can we do? I don't know what to do!" wailed Betty Fuller, her two-hundred-fifty pounds pacing about the room in search of a way to go.

"Let him stand on a table," somebody said. And they did.

"Not high enough," said Betty. So they got a chair, and put it on top of the table, and invited him to go up, and he did, from which loft he surveyed the room.

"How do you like it up there?" said Betty, craning up at his head near the ceiling.

"Fine," said he. And he did.

"Well," said Betty, "now that you're up there, tell us what's wrong with each one of us. . . . That's right. Go around the room and tell us what you think."

He started at his left and moved clockwise. For every person in the room he had a word. One was too this, another too that. He judged each in turn, told each what to do to be saved. After advising the last, he stopped.

"How does that feel?" said Betty.

"Fine," he answered. And it did.

She said nothing then, and there was a long pause. The judged people waited upon the judge.

He went round again, adding a bit here and a bit there for certain ones to whom he had not said quite enough. They nodded, and again there was silence.

Well? What do you do after judgment day? Tap dance? He didn't know how. He had come to the edge of history (he would read William Thompson's book of that title later) and he didn't know how to get back from the precipice. "History," he thought, "is the art of brinksmanship," and for the first time he saw a bit of himself in John Foster Dulles.

"Would you like to come down?" said Betty.

"Yes."

"Well, how could you get down?"

Stupid question. "I could get down the same way I got up."

She said nothing. He was like Didi and Gogo at the end of Beckett's play: he did not move.

The exercise of his power to judge everybody had discharged his animal energy. He was quiet now in all his large muscles, but he was not yet ready to rest. Nor was he going to climb down the same way he got up. Why not he didn't know. Absurd. He only knew he would not climb down. So he stood there and waited, and began to grow uncomfortable. After a while Betty broke the silence.

"All right. Turn around and face the wall. Close your eyes." He did so.

He was aware of Betty gesturing silently to the others. She was taking charge, and that suited him. Even so, and even though he had guessed what she was up to, he was not prepared for the effect her next words would have upon him.

"Fall backward," she said.

It was as if a poor soldier had heard his commander say, "Charge!" It meant now or never.

It was as if you were in a dream fleeing pursuers at your back and you came to a chasm you had to jump. You would either do it or not do it.

He had a clear sense of the room. It was no longer nondescript. It became as important to him as any room he had ever been in.

"You will," he thought to himself, "either do it or not do it."

He fell through water. Backward he went and down. Slow, the way parachutists say they experience the free fall of their sky-dive. He was diving backward. It might have been a thousand feet. The air turned to water as he sank. He did not gasp or cry or wriggle, nor think once about the solid floor. He fell into the waiting arms of people as into the sustaining pressures of some ocean deep. Arms cushioned his fall, received his weight, and held. They wafted him and brought him slowly to rest on the bottom.

He opened his eyes. He was looking up at faces. Big Betty Fuller was sitting on her heels, knees on floor, her long dress spread out over her great lap. He moved to put his head there and be held in her arms.

Then real water flowed. It welled in his eyes and began to run down his nose and cheek. He had no impulse to stop it. His diaphragm began to quiver, tremble, then convulse in large, wavelike movements. His lungs began to heave. Moans rose out of him, and he wept.

So there was nothing to say. After a time the waves subsided, and a few images drifted in his mind. The one he was most conscious of was his descent through water. It seemed, too, that the people were water, and he could swim in them. The word that drifted along with this image was *baptism*. He felt that he had once been baptized with sprinkling and now, here, in the Unitarian church, he had been baptized by immersion.

He did not mention this then. He left it to Betty Fuller to use words. When his crying stopped and he sat up, she said, "I feel so much pain in you, and it hurts me." He believed her. He realized that there is such a thing as vicarious suffering, which he had always thought to be a doctrine and a literary idea and now recognized as a feeling. The doctrine depended on the feeling, and you could not substitute the one for the other.

They all began to get up, and Betty Fuller suggested a break. He moved toward his wife and said, "Let's go out for a walk." They had both been so drained that they walked in silence most of the time. They went aimlessly around one block and another in that part of San Francisco, happy that it was night and dark and they needed to pay attention to no one. He walked through years of his marriage and noticed that it did not need his management. He was aware of the pain in it and knew that she was. He had tried to control, eliminate the pain by setting some kind of warning-posts around it. "Avoid This Area." "Quicksand Here." "Don't Go Near the Water." "Caution." Now he was wet. It felt better than dry.

At last he said to her: "These tears. Do you think they're what it's all about?"

"Yes," she said, "I do."

They were gone more than an hour. When they came back, the workshop had resumed. The group's attention was on another couple. The waters rolled on.

Five years had passed, to the month. The theologian looked up from his writing. She sat in a chair opposite, in a green tunic and black shorts. She was reading a book and taking notes. He looked at the bare parts of her skin, the shape of her crossed legs, the study in her eyes as she pondered some detail of what she read. She was for him that part of life most living. He loved her.

Almost everywhere you looked today tradition and change were squared off against each other, and those who passed for wise (or at any rate clever) were those who could manage the adjustments between them. The mandarins were the "crisis managers," as Roger Hillsman, once one of their number among the Democrats, had called them.

As the preoccupation with Communism vs. Freedom had divided the world into two and blinded the culture for years to the existence of a Third World that didn't care to take one side or the other but had a different, more immediate agenda, so the obsession with tradition vs. change blinded us to a third realm which, once seen, cast the whole into a new pattern. To this realm the theologian had been gradually awakening ever since his watery fall in San Francisco.

He did not want to say that a personal experience of repentance and love can resolve or replace the social exigencies. God help us.

He did not want to say that he had found peace in San Francisco and lived happily thereafter. Far from it.

He did mean, however, that public and personal were not separate spheres. If you saw this, you might also see how "tradition" and "change" were fictions. In the third realm, the radiance of God is now. You had not so much to judge as to breathe and swim.

Oh, that long history of theology, struggling ever and again to bring order to the emotions, correcting the excesses of "enthusiasm," rising to visions of God constant above the flux of passion. Oh, theology, great consort of Reason and political wisdom, bringing passion to stand penitent before truth and justice. Oh, divine revelation, destroying the fickle gods by the truth of the One, eternal sovereign, steadfast forever. Would he now cast that over, refuse custody of such a tradition, all for the sake of the felt life?

But what choice had he? For the minute he said yes to custody and control he put God in opposition to flux. And the flux is life.

He had every choice. He was standing now on the table and chair of his own tradition. He was standing on the shoulders of Paul Tillich, that great translator of "the eternal truth of the Christian message," the one he had chosen for seeming best to mediate between tradition and change. From this height, the theologian knew that he should fall.

"Fall backward," she had said. Who was big Betty Fuller now? What satanic voice tempted him to cast himself down? Women's voices, surely. They with their consciousness raising, their constant appeals to experience, their distrust of the Word of God, their critique of the theological tradition as chauvinist. Into what morass did they beckon him?

He would do it or not do it.

Kenosis. Emptying. But that was a Jesus trip. Like Eliot's Becket, he might do the right thing for the wrong reason.

So be it. He fell.

He might as well have been Gloucester in *Lear*, taking the blind plunge over Dover cliff and landing where he started, on the stage of the Globe Theater. No water, no height, no distance. It was no more possible to fall out of the tradition than for Shakespeare's actor to fall from ground zero. Then he thought of Betty Fuller once more, how he had told her what it meant to him when he had taken the plunge at her beckoning that night in San Francisco. "Such a fool thing to do," she said. "I thought you were crazy."

It was mid-day again. The birds were still singing. The day-lilies had opened, and he noticed how they were not toiling nor spinning. "Don't push the river," said Fritz Perls. "It flows by itself."

If it was not possible for him to fall out of the tradition, if he could not plunge through it the way the fellow in *Hair* "fell through a hole in the flag," still he need not hold on. Like the protagonist in Paul Goodman's *The Empire City*, "he touched his body and looked around and felt, 'Here I am and now'."

God, Self, and Authority

WALKING into Lampman Chapel that day, I had no signal of the chaos to come.

We had taken to meeting in Lampman because it was smaller than the high-ceilinged, rattly-windowed old 205 where we had started our work. I conduct the course, called "The Word of God as Human Experience," more like a workshop than a lecture course or a seminar. We use no furniture. The floor is our great leveler. The early part of the first semester is given to exercises, fantasies, meditations, and discussions aimed at increasing each person's self-awareness. This work is based partly on techniques of Gestalt therapy, which (by the way) is less a therapy than a process of growth and creativity. I have found it of much educational value.

Gradually our work comes to focus on specific texts and passages from books, all having to do with the topic, the Word of God. Prior to discussing these, we often play dramatic games with them. Some, especially from the Bible, are so glazed over with dull familiarity that we first burlesque them, to make them strange, to burst the bonds of old associations and interpretations, to get distance and perspective. While a few students object to this deliberate assault on seriousness, we have found that the texts soon spring back to assert a new claim on our attention, much as the musical *Godspell*, for instance, even as it burlesques the Gospel of Matthew, brings about listening to the words as if hearing them for the first time.

Other texts that we use are so unfamiliar, and some so abstract, that we dramatize them to lay hold of their ideas, structure, and argument. I may, for example, ask the students to draw up a list of *dramatis personnae,* treating the ideas the author uses as if they were to be the characters in a play. Then we group these according to affinities and antagonisms. Some ideas go with others like servingmen, companions, twins, etc., while others are sworn enemies, and so on. This seen, we go on to imagine the plot of the play, the story of the argument whereby the good ideas win, the bad ones lose, or they all get put in their place to live happily ever after, or whatever the case may be. Then we take to our feet and act out the script, improvising the dialogue. At this stage, the cogency of the author's appeal is severely tested, for if he or she has not convinced the students or made the matter clear, they will rewrite the argument as they proceed, sometimes improving it and sometimes leading it to a conclusion far different from the one the author foresaw.

Throughout this process, we find ourselves discovering not only what is in the book and what we think about it but also our basic affective response to it. One's feelings about a book, the pleasure and discomfort one gets from reading it, are in the long run quite as important as to understand it, for if the feelings are not strong the book will fade from memory, or the retained impression will probably be faulty. Far from encouraging, in this course, a detached objectivity such as some people call scholarly (and I call pedantic), I go for the opposite: a close, involved, passionate engagement with the mind and the words of the author. In this regard, to have a fervent dislike of a text is just as educational as to fall in love with it, provided the student is encouraged to carry the dislike to its limit. I have on occasion advised a student who claimed to hate a certain book to throw it straight out the window. No student has yet done so. I do not think the motive for restraint is only that of social propriety, nor even proprietary interest in the book's resale value. It seems to be closer to my own reaction to Karl Barth. I don't savor his theology, and yet I keep rereading it from time to time. In part, I *enjoy* reading Barth, to remember what I don't think. In part, I know there is something in his theology that I have not yet digested.

Lampman Chapel is a room about fifteen feet wide by thirty long. Like the whole of Union Seminary's quadrangle, it is in collegiate Gothic style. Along one side are a few stained-glass windows. The main door, at the rear, opens to a foyer. A smaller side door gives entry from a hallway. Near this door, the room is crossed by an altar rail, beyond which, up one step, are pulpit, lectern, and altar table. The space is intimate and quiet. It is often used for meditation and small services at early morning, vespers, or late evening. Since it was free on Monday afternoons, and because it was cozy for our class of seventeen persons, we took it over. We could easily remove and put back the few chairs in the place, and we found a number of small carpets to cover the tile floor.

One of our group, named Earl, objected to our using a sanctuary for the sometimes irreverent games we played; but he was overruled by the rest, who thought it no offense to do whatever we liked there, especially as our work seemed both religious and educational, however ludicrous in some respects. Earl was, in truth, only the most conventional of a whole range of pieties represented in the class. In fact, one of the functions of the course is to find out where the pieties are. We all have some, but they are not the same for everybody. Even the most skeptical and rebellious members of any theology class will have certain ideas, values, or practices that are, for them, untouchable and therefore sacred. For Earl, this quality adhered to Bible and church, which made him seem like a Fundamentalist to most of the other students, though in my eyes he seemed merely naive, unquestioning. Other students treated other things as sacred. For some, it was "truth" (about which they remained purposefully vague), or "love," or "service," or "ministry," or "the person." And for almost all, as we shall see, a sacred, unthinkable quality surrounded not the name but the activity of God. Which surprised me, so used was I to the veneer of skepticism so many theology students display.

The particular session I now recall, which included a terror quite unforgettable, took place one Monday in November. I had, I repeat, no idea what was coming. In my preparations for this course, I make up what I call a scenario—games to be played concerning the text or topic for the day, the order they will come in, their essential ingredients, the ideas I have that I want to communicate, one way or another, during the session. This creates a more or less open structure in which there is always room left free for the students to react and improvise as they will. The class plan is like a grid on which the students locate themselves and fill in the spaces that interest them; and this is how most of their learning takes place. In advance, I always try to imagine how I think the open spaces will be used, for I do not like to propose an activity that I think will leave people adrift nor one that seems irrelevant. I am often surprised by what does happen, but I have never been as taken aback as I was by the events of this particular Monday afternoon.

The session began with a challenge to my authority. This did not surprise me at all, for one of the features of the course is that *all* authorities, including those of personality and conviction, are tested and probed. To put myself on the floor with the students, to abandon the podium and the head of the seminar table, and yet to remain the teacher and leader of the class is to create an especially ambiguous situation. I suppose in a way I am playing Jesus, for the students soon begin to ask, "By what authority does he teach?" However, I certainly am not Jesus and do not have an evangelist writing about me in such a way that the answer to that question is obvious. So I frequently, in the face of the question, find myself asking *sotto voce* (and here I dare think that something similar occurred to Jesus), "By what authority *do* I teach?"

It has been important to me in my learning while teaching to find out that the authority question, as I call it, admits of no final answer. The situation is not unlike that of a parent, try as I may to avoid paternalism toward my students. In order to achieve his or her own legitimate authority, a growing child comes to a stage at which he or she asks (perhaps not in so many words), "Who gave *you* the authority to be my parent?" The question is terribly important because none of the obvious answers—God, nature, society, history, fate—does justice to the psychological and ethical profundity of it. More than almost any other question I can think of, it expresses the heart of what Tillich called "the Protestant principle," which does not, of course, mean Protestant*ism*. The question expresses the genuine protest of all inner authority against all that is extraneous. Most of us are middle-aged, and many live and die, before coming to the only mature answer. If I ask of my father and mother, as I did for many years whenever I felt judged or thwarted by them, "Who gave *you* the authority to be my parents?" the genuine answer must come from my own lips: "I did."

The question of another's authority is, *mutatis mutandi*, the question of my own authority. That is why no passing of the buck to "higher authority" will suffice. When my students say, "What makes you think you're the teacher here, because we all have selves and experiences as authentic as yours?" it is not on target to say that the school has appointed me a professor, or that my course requirements are backed up by warrant of the Dean's office, although these are certainly facts of life not entirely irrelevant. Neither does it hit the mark to claim that I have a certain knowledge of the materials, so and so many years of experience teaching them, certain pedagogical skills, books and articles to my name, and the like. Those again are matters of institutional credibility, having to do with my right to be (that is, be called) a professor and to have a professor's salary and prerogatives. But the judgments that led to this state of affairs were not made by the students in front of me and do not reach the heart of the matter. The students do not much care whether I *am* a professor, for that is not their responsibility (unless they should want to have me fired, which hasn't yet come up). What they want to know is whether I can *do* what I *am*, and in particular whether I can do it with *them*. To which the answer, of course, is that sometimes I can and sometimes I can't. So the question is never quite laid to rest. Besides, underneath the question about *me* is the question they are asking about themselves: "Are we ready to grant you the authority that you claim? And even if we did so week before last, when you were pretty good, you were not that good a week ago, and are we ready to do it today, here, now, when Lord knows what is about to happen?"

I began the session that day, as I often do, by asking if there were any feelings or unfinished business that anyone wanted to deal with before we went on. Someone, I don't remember who, raised the authority question. I don't even remember how. Alert to it, I went into one of my reflex positions. Half of me knew to take the objection seriously and stay open to it. The other half wanted off the hot seat. I can be very defensive under criticism. My defensive half complained—inside, unspoken: "Haven't we been over this enough? Don't they know by now there's no solution? Good as this question is, I don't want to spend all year on it. The lesson plan for today is *very* good, and I'd like to go on to that."

So I balked, and put myself in conflict, thus proving the point that I did not know how to handle authority and was therefore not worthy of their trust. "Good Lord, this is childish stuff," I thought, "not worthy of a graduate curriculum in theology." (The parent, challenged, becomes more parental still.) I do not believe I said anything clear.

Meanwhile, the only thing that *could* be clear was clear to the students. I was in pain. My face, body, and tone showed it, but I was unaware. To have known then and there that I was in pain would have required (in my mind) admission of failure. ("He teaches others to put their authority on the line, but himself he cannot do it.") So I pretended to be cool while my posture became contorted without my notice.

We were sitting in a circle. Opposite me was Lee. She had come to seminary highly and warmly recommended by her undergraduate teacher, who was a close friend of mine. Ever since September I had been realizing how strong and intuitive a person she is. Now she looked at me intently, and I realized she had something important to say.

"Tom," she ventured, "you talk as if the things we are saying don't matter to you." I shook my head to deny it. "But I believe," she went on, "that you are in pain. You seem not to want to show us your vulnerable side. It would help if you did."

I stared at her. Then very slowly my body softened. I began to notice how I was holding onto my legs. I started to sense that old, familiar pain in my left shoulder muscle, where I seem to send tension to be stored. In my chest I began to feel sorrow, for myself, who understand so much and yet cannot arrange life to suit me. And here was I, six months into my favorite, celebrated course about experience, still not knowing how to react honestly in a situation of challenge. My eyes began to water. I thought of all the circumstances of my life in which I do not handle authority well. I realized I knew very little of what my teen-age children think of me as a parent. I recalled my abuses of that authority and my lack of certainty about when I use it right. I thought of the tough front I often put up toward my wife. I remembered how difficult it is for me to be around persons who are powerful in institutions, how I tend to treat them as father figures. I thought of the many "mothers" I have adopted in my life, and how I rebel against them once adopted. Then, most painful stab, I remembered how many students in time past had told me that I frightened them.

All these thoughts came swift as a waterfall into the troubled pool of my mind. They poured down in a current of fear and sadness. Yet it is not possible fully to feel fear and sadness at the same time. I was aware then of a new conflict—whether to face my fear or to allow my sadness to come forth, as it had already started to do from my tear ducts. My body was tensing again.

I looked around the circle of students and realized that the main thing I was feeling in their presence was fear. If I lost control, what would the course become? My left shoulder screeched with pain. It told me I had "shouldered" a responsibility far beyond my power. Secretly, I had taken on the role of *the* authority in that room. Yet, given the way I had chosen to conduct the course, that could not be claimed. In a world where feelings count and where the testimony of experience matters, no authority can rule over others all the time. I believed this, and it frightened me. If the course got out of hand, if it turned out badly, what would become of my reputation? What would happen to me?

Across the circle, Lee sat in calm expectancy, waiting for me to speak. The others were waiting, too.

"I am frightened," I said. They nodded.

"Of what?"

I swallowed. "Of losing control."

"Are you about to?" asked Lee.

"I think so."

"Control over what?"

"Over you." I gestured to the whole circle. "Over this course."

"We don't need to be controlled," said someone. "We like this course, and we like you."

"I think," said Jean, "you are just controlling yourself." Then they all started to laugh. I began to shake. At first it was still the fear, and I trembled. Then it was a sort of shaking out, and my left shoulder began to bob. Then my belly started shaking, and I joined in the general guffaws.

"You must be a terrible person!" someone yelled with glee. "You have to control yourself all the time!" And the whole room shook with laughter such as I imagine is seldom heard in Lampman Chapel. When it died down, Lee spoke again.

"Tom," she said, "the only time we question your authority is when we don't know what you feel. When we know *you* can be hurt, then we're not afraid. Don't you see?" This last question was like her signature. As usual, she repeated it, tilting her head and screwing up her face as if to bore the obvious truth right through my defenses: "Don't you see? Don't you *see?*"

I smiled. "I do when you tell me," I said.

She threw back her head playfully and then tossed it forward: "Well, I *told* you!" Then she got up on her knees and crawled across the rug and threw her arms about me. We played for a minute like two puppy dogs, and the episode was over.

"OK," said somebody, looking at me, "what are we going to do today?" (Whew! I was back in control. Little did I know.)

We had read for the day a passage from Martin Luther's *Table Talk*. Chapter 35. There, Luther declares that in Christian worship it is "God himself [who] preaches, threatens, reproves, affrights, absolves, administers the sacraments, etc." Like much of Luther's writing, the passage is inherently dramatic, and I had decided that it would be an easy text to act out. I thought it would provide a good opportunity for the students to see how they viewed themselves as present or future "servants of the Word of God," especially as preachers who might stand, as Luther clearly wanted, under the authority of the Scriptures. Luther is good on this subject because his manner of obeying scriptural authority is never obsequious. On the contrary, he is very self-assertive, which posture gives rise to the drama in his authorship.

I now proposed acting out the text, and the class conveyed, if not great eagerness, at least assent. So I quickly ran through the cast of characters, which was fairly obvious, and said that the first character to be cast was God. I asked for a volunteer.

At this moment the real drama of the afternoon began, or rather failed to begin, for we entered upon a very dialectic situation in which, as in much modern theater, action appeared as nonaction.

There were no immediate volunteers for the role of God. The request was not being greeted with refusal but with tentativeness. My surprise started here, for the role of God in the Luther passage is not complicated, and I had foreseen that all the casting would go quickly. That was because I had not anticipated that the real hang-up of the class, including myself, was over authority. I had only to mention the word *God* to involve everyone in the same problem I thought we had just got through.

While we waited for the volunteer, I could see muscles twitching in many persons in the room. I did not know who would make the first deliberate movement. I decided not to volunteer myself, for I wanted very much to observe the process. So I sat back, something like a God beyond God, to see what would happen.

After a few moments, Susan volunteered. I could see her going through the motions that looked like making up her mind, and soon she edged herself into the center of the circle—somewhere off-center, that is, for she actually moved only a foot or two.

"I guess I'll do it," she said in a voice full of hesitation.

"Good," I thought. "We'll have a female deity, and that may bring something to the matter that Luther did not imagine." I knew that Susan was very conscious of

women's issues and was considering ordination in the Episcopal church. To see her hesitant, however, was new, for
she is usually the soul of courage.

Well, now we had a God. Or did we? Susan looked very
unsure of herself, the more so as no one (except Sally, who
beamed her approval of a woman on the heavenly throne)
made any response to Susan's having broken the ice. So
Susan said, to anyone who might answer, "Do you want me
to do it?"

"What's this?" asked Jean. "Is God asking for permission
to be God?"

"I guess so," said Susan. "Will I do?"

We let her fry. She moved as if to return to her former
place, thought better of it, went back a little closer to the
center, looked around again, backed off, finally slumped in a
place indecisive. No one could tell whether she was going to
be God or not.

Then a discussion began. Not vigorous, not clean or focused, just a lot of comments and questions and mutterings
about what she was doing, and how much support did she
need, and who or what is God anyway, and did anyone else
want to volunteer, and did people want to prop up this
Susan God, which would surely mean entering into some
sort of covenant with her when she hadn't yet done anything and they didn't really know if they wanted her or not.

This went on a long time. It was very frustrating, and I
would have attempted to cut it off if most of the class had
not seemed to have so much negatively invested in it. I
could sense a lot of energy among the people, though none
of it came out directly. I expected one of the men to try and
settle the "women's question" once and for all by upstaging

Susan and becoming God himself. There was clear opportunity to demonstrate that God is masculine because women don't know how to do anything, but this did not happen. Instead, the group fixed itself in a paradigm of the "what if" situation, like a person who stands by a pool unable to decide to jump in. The whole class was now at the water's edge, looking as if it would stay there forever. Equally surprising was the fact that no one changed the subject or wandered out of the room. All were involved with their noninvolvement, and so was I. The situation, which can paralyze a group as well as an individual, is called by Fritz Perls "the hanging on bite." He has another image for it, too. He speaks of the person who will "neither shit nor get off the pot."

I wondered if the group was punishing me for my own ambivalence about authority. But no one looked at me, and I decided they were punishing themselves at least as hard, so I would see how long they kept it up. Meanwhile, I pondered my old, always fascinating question: "How does *anything* get started?"

Then came the scream. I hear it yet. Blood-curdling. I did not see it prepared, and I think no one, not even the screamer, knows when it started to rise. It was so loud it seemed to come from all over the room. I think my head turned once in the wrong direction before I looked to my left (away from Susan) to see Bill—the scream still shrieking from his throat, his face and neck red as from apoplexy, his hands high over his head in a gesture of agony, his eyes wild as a beast—hurl himself to the floor, toss once, and lie as if dead.

I had but an instant to decide whether he needed first aid. I decided not, and remained motionless, a God beyond God in utter impassivity. The room was still for a few seconds of shock.

Then came the second scream. From Jill. It was to me nearly as frightening as the first, and to some people more so. It was, I soon realized, the sound of a genuine hysteria.

In those days, Jill was frequently on the verge of hysteria, though I had never seen her succumb before. She was one of those brilliant people who seem always about to explode. The presence of such a person in my class, and I always have one or two, for I decline to screen them out, offered plenty of excuse for me to believe in the importance my being always in control. I kept a certain psychological distance from Jill. I did not want to become, as I imagined she wished, her faculty mentor, for fear of having a "case" on my hands. "Let her spread it around," my instinct had told me. She had long been in therapy, but the tide of her development had not yet turned very strongly in the direction of stability and health. That was to come later. Now, as I had feared, she had gone far out of control. The scream that came from her was born of panic. Seeing Bill crash to the ground, she believed him dead or dying, as she told us later; and this, plus the preceding hemming and hawing of the group, had triggered her fears of chaos and death. I read terror on her face, and a desperate desire to be helped.

The two screams piercing the air one after the other stirred up a storm in the room. Some persons nearest Bill bent over him to see if he needed rescue. Some others, mostly women, made for Jill, who continued to scream, wail, beat her fists, shake her head in a frenzy, and writhe like one possessed. I decided to remain where I was. I knew that the persons who now surrounded Jill and were trying to hold her knew as much as I about hysteria, perhaps more. Jill seemed aware of her surroundings, and I judged that she could survive whatever ordeal she was going through. I sat and kept watch, ready to send for help if necessary.

Pandemonium broke out. I wish I had had a TV pack (we did use one in some of our sessions) to record the scene, though I am sure I would have been mugged if I had tried to use it at that moment. In one degree or another, the hysteria spread to everyone in the room, especially those not attending directly to Bill or Jill. All except the two patients, their nurses, and me were now on their feet. A wild energy seemed to invade the bodies and send them ricocheting in space. I could not keep track of everyone. To Jill's continuing cries were added shouts and exclamations of all kinds. Earl took to his knees in the middle of the room and began fervently to pray, voicing his petitions upward through the general din and raising his eyes to heaven as if to see whether any of his appeals arrived there. This behavior made others angry. Some moved in circles around him, with shouts and threatening gestures. It was as if his pious response to emergency was seen as something demonic, or that it evoked the demonic in *them*. The women attending Jill were particularly offended. One after another, they would raise their heads to snarl and growl. Ted was very frightened and behaved like a cat unable to escape from the vicinity of a dogfight. He moved here and there finding no place to hide, wondering what on earth to do with himself. Paul became a prophet, as I gradually realized, though at first he impressed me as a traveling windmill. He dashed everywhere, taking large, rapid strides while rotating his arms in great circles.

He would fly up into the pulpit area and then traverse the length of the room to go straight out the doors at the back, then reappear with the same momentum while the door was still swinging, this time zig-zagging his way to the altar, then out the door again in a long, straight line, and so on ceaselessly. Finally, he climbed up and stood on a window-sill, from where he proclaimed the Day of the Lord. No one but me paid him the slightest attention. The awesome activity in the room had no focal center whatever. From time to time, Jill lifted her head toward me and screamed, "Why don't you help me?," to which I replied, "You have plenty of help already." Then she would return to her crying and gradually let the others comfort her.

The bedlam continued for about half an hour. I sat wondering how long it would go on. Having been set off in one instant, like a flame in kerosene, it was out of control. I judged that I might be able to stop it if I suddenly got up and demanded attention, but I wasn't sure. Even to *get* attention would have been hard amid that cyclone. Meanwhile, I again noticed that nobody fled the room, which told me that the explosion I was watching had some kind of magnetic attraction. There were moments when I came close to panic myself, for I had no idea what was going on or would come next. And always I had the fear that some physical or psychological damage might occur, to injure not only a victim but also to prove to my detractors' satisfaction that I had no business conducting this kind of a course. What residue, I wondered, of this day's trauma would Jill have to cope with at home alone? Were there others in the room who might really flip out?

I decided to assume whatever risk there might be. I have come to hold the view that Christianity often goes wrong in protecting people from themselves. This is a great pitfall for those who take up "the ministry." In the name of love, service, altruism, persons are coddled. "Helping others" comes to mean anticipating danger *for* them. Two bad results follow: the "others" are treated like children, and the "helpers" become so concerned with preventing what *might* go wrong in the world that they do not alleviate the *actual* suffering in it. For this reason, I now resisted my temptations to interfere, which in any case would have been mostly to still my own panic. I let the scene run its course.

As I said, the storm blew for some thirty minutes. Then gradually it subsided. Energies were spent. The noise died down, motion slowed and stopped. Jill went on sobbing a little without sound. Some people stopped where they were, still standing. Others lay on the floor like rag dolls, or sat in a slump. All the eyes were dazed. Sweat dripped from foreheads. Kerchiefs came out of pockets. Hair fell disheveled from the tops of heads. I wondered if this is what it is like at the end of an orgy. Some kind of an orgy this had surely been. Without a word, people started going out of the room. When I heard the sound of the lavatory door being opened across the hall, I realized they were going to relieve themselves and wash up. I myself went for a walk.

After a few minutes, I returned, and so did everyone else except Bill, and Paul, who had followed him. They came back later.

The circle re-formed. Silence.

"Well," said I. "What was that?"

They asked, "What did it look like?"

I replied, "To me, it looked like"—I paused—"chaos."

They said, "It *was* chaos."

Then we sat again in silence for a time. Ever since, the episode has been known as Chaos Day.

I asked Jill what had happened to her. She answered, "I was frightened. So frightened." She began again to shudder. "I thought that Bill was dead. I was afraid of everything going wrong, and I was afraid that I would die. I was angry at you because you wouldn't help me."

I smiled. "I thought that you could survive without me."

She smiled back, though her face still showed some anger and hurt. "I guess so. I guess I did." The shudder again. "I never felt like that before."

There followed a general discussion about Bill's "death," which had so startled everyone. Some had thought he was really stricken, and they could not understand how anyone could have reacted otherwise. Others said it was phony though convincing. They had been set off more by Jill than by Bill. But since his scream was revealed to have been an act, what was behind it? He, sly fellow, was now out of the room. When he returned, he disclosed that the "performance" was unpremeditated release from his own exasperation. He had suffered the group's indecision over God or no-God as long as he could. "I didn't know what to do," he said. "I just wanted something to happen."

How does *anything* get started?

What follows now is the gist of the discussion with which we ended the day. Because I cannot remember the dialogue, and because the ideas are close to my heart, I put them in my own words. I should perhaps report that Jill, although she took a very clear part in the discussion, did not return to class again. Her fear was too great, her psychological balance too unstable. She came to me a day or so later and said she wanted to withdraw. Could I arrange a way for her to complete the course without attending? We worked this out, and she wrote the paper we devised. Since then, she turned a corner. She is now so healthy and cheerful I rejoice when I see her. But that's another story.

The chaos was real. Well, of course, there's always the philosophical question whether there's any reality to chaos, since it lacks structure and function; but the episode was about as chaotic as could be imagined short of actual destruction. Although it was a simulation, it was not intentionally so; and although no one went crazy, still no one knew very much about what they were doing or why. The scene looked from the outside, and was felt from the inside, to be chaotic. Such structure as it had was like a parody of structure. As for function, it had none except the disspelling of frustrated energies. I do not think that in any but a very vague sense it was therapeutic for anyone. It was, however, frightening; and this fact we later used as something to reflect upon.

When I look at the day as a whole, however, I do see a structure, one that seems to me far from accidental, even though nobody planned it. The day started with a stab at the authority question. Who's in charge here, why and how? We resolved this in a certain way, but the ensuing events say to me that we did not resolve it at a very deep level, if in fact it *can* be resolved. At any rate, the authority question cannot be laid to rest by any pure insight but must find its resolution in action. Since it did not do this in the first part of the afternoon, it got carried over.

The second episode hinged upon my asking for a volunteer to play God. As I've already noted, this amounted (though I was at the time too blind to see it) to an escalation of the authority question as far as it could go. God is your great initiator—in the Luther passage and in much religious imagination. The volunteer I was asking for would have to take the initiative to become the initiator. Not only that: he or she would have to do so in a "void," not knowing how to play the role. That also would have to be initiated. Thus, the image of God as one who creates-out-of-nothing coincided with the sense of self as one who either will or will not assume responsibility, make an act with structure and consequences unforeseen. From this, I imagine, came the group's hesitation, which Susan dramatized by volunteering and not volunteering at the same time.

The "authority question," which the group had at first externalized by focusing it upon me (not that I didn't deserve it) was now transposed. Having agreed to go along with my game for the day, and not having overtly rebelled at my request for a volunteer, the group now had to wrestle with its own authority, both as a group and individually. The question of authority, which on its external side is a "political" question (who's in charge here?), now moved to its internal side and became the question of authorship and authenticity. The two sides are related, the reason why political questions are also psychological and moral questions, and vice versa.

When Susan failed to authorize herself courageously in the role of God, and when the group refused the anomaly of doing it for her, the stage was set for chaos. The fear that something bad might happen was balanced by the fear that nothing would happen. Stalemate. Not inert, however, for the potential energy was high. In fact, the situation, though it looked very dull, was highly charged, as the succeeding episode proved. The potential energy, which I watched in the behavior of twitching muscles, provided the impulse to act, even though this was thwarted by fear of unknown responsibility. No one, at that moment, would "own" anything. The action, as I said earlier, was nonaction.

What was God doing on the day before creation? Augustine said such a question is illogical because time and the creation start together, so there *was* no day before. That is logically correct, provided we think abstractly; but no act is logical in that sense. None is imaginable without a gathering and focus of energy. One, two, three—go! Before the pitch, the wind-up. This we recognize in all actions we notice in the structured world. And before there *was* a world? Before the first action of any? This "before" is odd, as Augustine said. But the book of Genesis, like most creation myths, is clear about it: before the first action, chaos.

Chaos is not nothing. It is, of course, no *thing*, in that sense nothing. But it is the potential for action. I have to imagine that on the day before creation God felt the stirring of potential from within. An initial act is mysterious enough anyway. I do not need to make it totally capricious by thinking that it has no preparation, no intentionality, no coming together of imagination and force. On the day before creation, I fancy, God was like Susan at the edge of the circle. His muscles, or whatever he has in place of muscles, twitched. If God is female, her womb contracted. Certainly, in the myth we have, God took counsel, as Susan did when she asked if we wanted her to be God. This is the significance of the first-person-plural pronouns in the biblical story. They mean this even if, as I doubt, they are derived from the "royal we"; for the intent of that convention is to say that the king takes counsel with himself if not also his court. Such counseling or deliberation, such a hesitance between the impulse and the deed, is essential to an act. It means not only that the act aims to be purposeful and rational but that it will be an *act* and not a random gesture.

In the moment of hesitance the question of authorship arises. To become the author of an act is at once to do it and to take responsibility for doing it. Not only will the act be done (the passive voice evades responsibility, is parasitic on the active), but *I* do it. For better or worse. Every act is a covenant. Few people have understood the moment of hesitance better than W. H. Auden:

> But how shall we
> satisfy when we meet,
> Between Shall-I and I-will,
> The lion's mouth whose hunger
> No metaphors can fill?[1]

On Chaos Day, when Susan faltered, and the group faltered, and I played the God beyond God who never does

---

[1] "The Sea and the Mirror," from *The Collected Poetry of W. H. Auden* (New York: Random House, 1945), p. 351.

anything, we came to the lion's mouth. Its jaws had already been opened by "the authority question." It was very hungry. Bill, yelling out his exasperation and hurling himself down in a theatrical, ambiguous gesture, threw the lion a piece of raw meat. The jaws clamped down, catching Jill in their bite, and we all spent half an hour in the belly of the beast.

When we have a paradigm situation of the moment of hesitance—as in *Hamlet*, for instance, or in your life and mine many times—and when we neither claim authorship nor reject it, we are in chaos. We are then on the day before creation, afraid of the following day. We are lucky if the chaos does not erupt as it did in Lampman Chapel and at the court of Claudius in Denmark.

"What did it look like?"

"It looked like chaos."

"It *was* chaos."

That chaos is worst which is encountered without knowing, or without our being willing to acknowledge, that we stand on the day before creation. Among other things, God is the name of that standing. Because he not only stands (or *is*) but acts, he is called the Author. As such, I believe, he does not so much answer our "authority question" as to call it up. The only way in which he "answers" it is by "playing the game."

> when god decided to invent
> everything he took one
> breath bigger than a circustent
> and everything began

when man determined to destroy
himself he picked the was
of shall and finding only why
smashed it into because[2]

"And God said. . . ." It is like taking a big breath, and out
it comes. How does anything get started?

"And God said, 'Let there be . . .'" Let. Curious particle
of speech. Whatever does it mean? It's an imperative. To
whom is it addressed? The creative act, any genuine act,
springs from a void and makes its own world as it goes
along. "Let there be . . . and there was . . ."

Susan, thank you. For I saw in you that day the image of
God on the day before creation. You didn't quite make it,
and we fell deeper into chaos, but you taught me to wonder
how God made it, and I'm sure I don't know. I don't even
know how *I* make it, when I do.

Bill, thank you. For you showed me that the ambiguous
gesture doesn't make it, either. Forceful you were, and a
new time you did precipitate; but you cared not what you
did, and having done it you "died." It was a superb moment
of theater, but it failed as drama. Out of it, unlike the action
of God, there came no plot, just fireworks till all the powder
was gone. Too easy, old fellow. Too easy, you raving King
Lear: "I shall do such things—/What they are yet I know
not, but they shall be/The terrors of the earth!" (II, iv, 11.
275–77).

Jill, thank you. For you showed me the chaos that fear of
chaos brings. When I saw you live through your chaos, I

---

[2] e. e. cummings, *Complete Poems: 1913–1962,* (New York: Harcourt,
Brace, Jovanovich, 1972), p. 566.

knew that its opposite is not order but courage. Tillich, you know, calls it the courage to be. I call it the courage to do. Your wails and your beating of fists were the most purposeful acts of the day. To cry from the depths is not to do nothing. Among your comforters, you cried to me like Job to God. And Job, not God, is the hero of that book.

In the beginning God created the heavens and the earth. The earth was without form, and void, and darkness was upon the face of the deep. . . .

And God said, "Let there be light"; and there was light. And God saw that the light was good; . . . (Gen. 1: 1–4).

Telling Time:
The Importance of Stories
and Theology's Tall Tale

A NUMBER of theologians recently have become interested in the importance of stories. They sense that all our logical, scientific, and theological discourse is secondary. Narrative is primary. I share this belief. I have long thought that theology is to religious narrative as literary criticism is to literature—commentary upon a more basic form of expression.

It is not my purpose in this chapter to expound upon the expositors of theology as story. Instead, I wish to add to the literature some thoughts about stories that are provided by the Gestaltist approach I have taken to theology. Gestalt theory aids me to reflect upon time, memory, and narrative. I launch this chapter with observations about stories as gestalts, and I will end it with a parable designed to warn us that while stories are essential and basic they are not the whole of life.

An event is a gestalt of motion. It is the figure of an occurrence. The point is perhaps redundant. A careful reader of my earlier chapters will have noticed that I believe all phenomena to be in motion, all perceptions dynamic. Every gestalt *is* an occurrence. What we experience as life is the flow of these. We speak, often enough, of "the river of life" and its current.

A story is the form whereby we connect one event with another to form a larger, more comprehensive gestalt. I sometimes call a story a "gestalt of gestalts." Like a history (the two words used to mean the same) a story is a pattern made up of a certain set of events. In stories the river of life becomes differentiated. It becomes not only flow but meaningful or structured flow.

"Where did you go?" runs the title of a book about children, the rest being as follows:

"Out."

"What did you do?"

"Nothing."

Children, who love to hear stories, can be exasperatingly vague when asked to tell a story about themselves. It takes a long time for one's identity to be clear enough to be seen as the subject of a story. As Penelope Gilliatt has remarked on the subject of children's responses to movies, "Details count for much more than narrative until quite late in life."[1]

[1] "Thoughts on Being a Child at the Movies," *The New Yorker* 51, no. 23 (28 July 1975): 49–50.

There is a positive correlation between knowing myself and telling stories about myself, or telling any story.

In *Aspects of the Novel*, E. M. Forster distinguished a story from a plot. The principle by which he did so is quite important, although Forster used "story" to refer to what I, following R. G. Collingwood and Benedetto Croce, would call a mere "chronicle." Here are Forster's famous passages:

A story is a narrative of events arranged in time sequence. (A story, by the way, is not the same as a plot. . . . The plot is an organism of a higher type. . . .)

A Plot is also a narrative of events, the emphasis falling on causality. "The king died and then the queen died," is a story. "The king died, and then the queen died of grief" is a plot. The time-sequence is preserved, but the sense of causality overshadows it.[2]

The "sense of causality," as Forster called it, turns the two events into a structured, unified whole. Two separate gestalts have now become one; and this is what I, unlike Forster, call a story. My usage agrees with that of the ten-year-old girl with whom Penelope Gilliatt discussed movies. Ms. Gilliatt asked her to describe a disaster picture she might make up, and was told about a tidal wave that would strike a narrow beach and wash away seven people, three ladies and four children, who would then swim to an island. Ms. Gilliatt reports: "When I wanted to know about the rest of the story, she explained that it wouldn't really be a story, it would just go on."[3]

---

[2] E. M. Forster, *Aspects of the Novel* (New York: Harcourt, Brace, and World, 1954), pp. 51, 130.
[3] "Thoughts on Being a Child . . ."

In common usage, I think "story" implies plot, which Aristotle (in the *Poetics*) said was the "soul" of a drama. Plot is the soul of any story that is not just a mere listing of events. Aristotle called the plot the soul or breath (*psyche*) of the story because the plot is invisible and yet animates and integrates the whole. A plot is something we either get or fail to get, like the point of a joke. No amount of describing the plot will put it into anyone's head unless the auditor on his or her own account will close the gestalt. This is one reason stories are felt to be mysterious, even sacred, and are so often associated with religious experience. To "get" a story is a kind of revelation.

The Greek word for "plot" used by Aristotle is *mythos*, which our language borrows as "myth." Even today there remains among us a certain awareness that all stories are myths. Unfortunately, both words have acquired a pejorative connotation. "Oh, that's just a story." Or, "That's only a myth." Were it not for stories and myths, however, we would never know more than cats and dogs about the river of life.[4] One thing would follow another ("one damn thing after another," as Will Rogers sardonically put it), none more meaningful than the next. The whole, if it did not breed cynicism, would take on the quality of *maya*, an illusion from which our souls need to be freed.

[4] This difference between animals and humans seems to me clearer than those usually mentioned—symbolic formation, speech, the use of tools, and so on. Whether animals are capable of learning any kind of human language is at present unclear, although it does seem that chimpanzees can learn to communicate using signs and symbols. In any case, people talk to animals and get results, even if they have to guess what is the animal's level of comprehension. What I have never heard of is evidence that an animal could understand (on any level) a story. = understand causality.

Here lies, if I understand the matter, a great difference between the religious philosophies of the West and the East. Christianity (like Judaism) is an historical religion because it holds that life is a story. We Westerners are a biographical people, and even our science does not shrink from attempting to discover the biography of the material universe. The stories of Hinduism and Buddhism, however, are imbued with an irony that undercuts their ultimate seriousness.

I think it will be much to the good if Christianity learns from Buddhism to take stories and histories with a grain of salt. We have tended to be rather obsessed with them. Since the Enlightenment, we have gone about diligently trying to separate the true stories (that is, history and science) from the myths. We have seemed determined to ferret out the one true "plot" of the universe. To the philosophers of the East, this Western obsession with beginnings, causes, and ends has seemed like a child forever trying to tie its shoelace.

"Don't push the river," said Fritz Perls, "it flows by itself." The attitude is Taoist. The river is the *tao*, the "way." It is "all," and it is finally not subject to our manipulations. Christianity knows of this in Jesus' reminder that the panoply of Solomon was not as glorious as the lilies of the field that "neither toil nor spin." He advised his followers to "take no thought for the morrow." Don't push the river.

If we compare Jesus with St. Paul, we may notice that while Jesus is a master storyteller and teaches hardly anything without a parable, Paul has turned the whole of history into a saga notoriously lacking in humor and irony. Paul's saga begins with Adam and Eve, since whom the "whole creation" has been "groaning" with labor pains until the coming of the Christ, who is about to come again and bring an end to all travail. This stupendous story overwhelms everything, and it is no wonder that Paul felt we "see as in a dark mirror." By comparison, even in John, not to mention the synoptics, Jesus trips the light fantastic. Ever since the New Testament epistles (and probably before) Christianity has felt tension between the lightness of its occasional stories, not to be taken too seriously, and its big story that beclouds the whole earth while trying to tell of its redemption.

If we learn lightly to tell stories and gently to play with them in our mind, then we may know how to read and hear them. I try to imagine how we might take our stories seriously enough and still not get hung up on them. We might then come to enjoy our theological stories, too, and not stone them to death with dogma.

Here are three thoughts about good stories I like to keep in mind: (1) They all take place in existential time; (2) in their beginning is their end; (3) they float on the river of life and do not dam it up.

There is a seemingly obvious notion that time proceeds in a straight line from past to present to future. Who would deny such a self-evident truth? Does not the phonograph needle start at the rim of the record and come, twenty minutes later, to the inside? Does not the acorn first become a sapling and then a big oak tree? Did not Athens flower before Rome, and both before Paris? Does not any good clock run only one way?

Yea, verily. But there is something else to be said, equally valid. Here is an example of it—Pozzo's famous outburst in Samuel Beckett's *Waiting for Godot*. Pozzo has just said that Lucky is dumb and cannot speak.

VLADIMIR: Dumb! Since when?

POZZO (*Suddenly furious*):   Have you not done tormenting me with your accursed time! It's abominable! When! When! One day, is that not enough for you, one day he went dumb, one day I went blind, one day we'll go deaf, one day we were born, one day we shall die, the same day, the same second, is that not enough for you? (*Calmer*) They give birth astride of a grave, the light gleams an instant, then it's night once more.[5]

Once. One day. Once upon a time.

I do not take Pozzo's outburst to mean that time is not important. On the contrary, to Pozzo time seems to matter—terribly. I take the speech to say there is something crucial about time you will never know by chronology.

Didi's "When?" springs from a conventional sense of time I will call chronological, the usual name for it. Pozzo's protest springs from a time-sense I will call, for lack of a better term, existential. Both are valid inasmuch as their usefulness depends on the function time is to serve in our thought. I hold, however, that chronological time is abstracted from existential time, and that the latter is prior in every sense of the word.

Perception of time, like all other perception, occurs in the

[5] Samuel Beckett *Waiting for Godot,* (New York: Grove Press, 1954), p. 57.

present.[6] All time is defined with respect to now. Language (and not only language) reflects this. Grammatically, the future tense and the past tense are variants of the present, their meanings relative to it. To understand that something was or will be, I have to understand, negatively, that the present has been excluded (or partly excluded) from the grammatical sense. The converse is not true. To understand "I breathe" requires no logical operation respecting the past or the future, while to understand "I did breathe" requires the logical intervention of an instruction in the computer of the brain: "Exclude, in principle, present reference."

Anticipation of the future is what gives urgency to the present. The more I wonder (not dread) what *will* happen, the more alert I stay now. There is thus a special affinity between present and future. The present *is becoming* the future. This continual transition from now to not-yet I call the present-future. All living beings exist in it, even those that have little memory. Movement into the future is what gives rise to the notion of the irreversibility of time.

[6] It is odd to speak of "perceiving" time. If we may perceive time, what is the organ of perception? While I do not wish to rest my case on it, I imagine that biologists will answer the question before long. There are probably special centers in the nervous system for detecting the passage of time. In any case, it is possible to suffer jet-lag. Our kinesthetic sense is now well known, although the details of its functioning are obscure. This sense provides to our brains information about our orientation in the gravity field. May we not also, especially since Einstein, speak of a time field? There is probably a literature on this I have not discovered. I am suggesting that just as we perceive spatial arrangements in a field of which our own sensory apparatus is the moving center, so we perceive temporal arrangements in a similar field.

Our relation to the past is different from our relation to the future, unless the freedom in us has been destroyed. In Eugene O'Neill's *Long Day's Journey Into Night,* Mary Tyrone, who is addicted to morphine, says, "The past is the present, isn't it? It's the future, too." This poignant line expresses time as fateful, but we recognize in it the motive of self-justification. Our past is our present-future *if* we do not now intervene. Can we, will we act? The question cannot be answered in the abstract. Mary Tyrone's caveat is that of a woman who has taken herself out of the game. She uses the past to rationalize her passivity in the present-future. Said Perls: "The traumatic event in the past is not the cause of a neurosis but its symptom."

Reflection along these lines has brought me to a certain gestalt I call the "time-loop." In this image, time starts in the present. (Time is here a function of the freedom to know and to act: existential time.) It moves headlong into the future. This movement is not, however, automatic. It is arrested by something I called in chapter 5 the "moment of hesitance." That means, a time of reflection when I anticipate the future and decide upon a course of action. This moment includes a threat of chaos. It is experienced as dreadful or creative or both. In such a moment, time loops "reflexively" upon the past, which is felt to hold clues or answers to the present dilemma. This process is clearest in the operation of reflexes subliminal to consciousness. If, when getting up from a chair, I start to fall, past-encoded reflexes go to work. Since I lack time to think in this emergency, the lower centers of my brain take over and do what they have learned to do in the past, righting my balance involuntarily. The invocation of the past as guide to the present-future is a conservative function, and without it we would not survive.

The social uses of traditions are, I believe, analogous to the conservative reflexes of our bodies. A tradition preserves whatever may need to be repeated (perhaps with modification) in the present for the sake of the future. Our political and social conservatism will be manifest in how much we try to repeat, how much we modify, and how much we repudiate for the benefit of our new situations.

The uses of history are both reflexive and reflective; reflexive repetitions to conserve the social fabric and reflective historical criticism for the sake of change.

To the extent that I treat the past as immutable ("What's done is done; the past is dead," etc.) I repeat it neurotically. The loop of time backward upon itself has not then been made with sufficient reflection. It turns forward again to the future, without passing through the moment of hesitance. In this way the past *does* become the future, into which we go more crippled than before. Instead of learning something new from our emergencies, we unthinkingly relearn the bad lessons that got us into the jam in the first place, like an alcoholic who cures a hangover with another drink, or a pianist who gets worse the more he practices because he reinforces an awkward fingering.

"Why is this man blind?" the disciples asked Jesus. "Who sinned?" They looked for causes, moral causes, in the past. Jesus replied. "Not because of his sins, or the sins of his parents, as you suppose, but that the works of God should come to light in him" (John 9:1–3). In other words: "The use of the past is not to explain or determine the present, but I and this man will now make use of his past for the sake of the Kingdom that is present-future."

"Well, that's not the way we've been doing things," I can imagine the Sadducees to reply. "Nor is it what our fathers taught."

"I know it," Jesus might come back. "I know as much about that as you do. You have heard it said. I do not destroy one jot or tittle of that. And *I* say and do something different."

The difference to which Jesus points is between a living history and a dead one. The difference emerges in what happens to our actions when the loop of existential time returns upon the present after its round into the past. For Jesus, as I read the Gospels, the past serves the present; to-day is the acceptable day of the Lord; the hour cometh and now is.

When? One day.

A certain man went down from Jerusalem to Jericho. When? One day.

We recognize in a parable that dates don't count. The parable, we say, states a universal truth, so time doesn't matter. But it does matter—first, because if it did not there would be no reason to state the truth in story form; second, because the hearer lives in time, and the story is to make him or her more aware of that. One day—this day—I am to meet my stranger neighbor in need by the wayside. The parable takes place *now*, in existential time. But so do all other stories, though we don't notice.

Suppose I start a story with the sentence, "In or about the year 30 A.D. Jesus of Nazareth was put to death by crucifixion near Jerusalem." Oh, fine, we may think. This is probably a true story, and it's about something that happened long ago. (Notice the present tense.) The story (any story) requires that I locate it with respect to myself now. Whether it is a true story or a fiction is a judgment I have to make now. No one else, not even the storyteller nor the story itself, can make this judgment for me; and I have to make it every time. This is because the story unfolds in my imagination, the contents of which require of me a continual "positioning" (or "intention" as Sartre would say) with respect to my present existing in the world. As long as I am sane, I do this regarding both the story's content and its time. An expression like "30 A.D." means, among other things, "so and so long ago." The story, existing in present-future time and in the imagination of the reader/listener, must be placed somewhere on the existential time-loop. We locate a "long-ago" story in the past in order to draw it forward again through the present as we proceed into the future. Otherwise it makes no sense, and we will either not "get" the story (as young children do not "get" history) or we say, "So what?" "Was there a dwarf in Caesar's army?" runs a familiar question designed to illustrate this point. Whether there was or wasn't is not yet a story, not history. To become so, it has to matter, and it has to matter now.

A story's presence *now* in the imagination of the listener is not, I believe, a merely philosophical point *about* the story, not simply commentary, but is an ingredient of the story itself. To be more accurate, a story does not exist in and of *words in book meaning*

Tree in forest sound

itself. The story happens in the encounter between the listener and a certain set of words. Like all words, these have no existence as *words* until someone reads, hears, and recognizes them. The story becomes story in a transaction between teller (or writer) and listener. Awareness of the story's coming to be is what makes a good story alive.

The creation of a vivified present is the prime motive for telling stories, and this becomes even more important in religious communities, where stories go hand in hand with making music, performing sacraments, and doing rituals of all kinds: "The hour cometh and now is." Rightly apprehended, these activities do not glorify the past so much as they fill the present with power. It is as if the energy of all time were trained upon the present, charging it with meaning, and causing it to burst with potency upon the future. A story and a religious ceremony, like sexual intercourse, all move to climax by conflating past and future into the present with such intensity that the gathered wave breaks. Then we plunge again into the amorphous waters of life.

This concentration upon the present—an act at once physical, psychological, and ideational—means that the story is or becomes a unity in which every part contains the whole. The story's end is in its beginning, and vice versa. Stories that lack this quality have either thwarted it for a deliberate esthetic effect (they are anti-stories) or they are flawed. "The king died," is by itself not the same as it will forever become with the addition of, "and the queen died of grief." The story is a gestalt, the unified image of the coherence of a set of events; and this gestalt is formed, as often as the story is told, in existential time.

Integrated and distinct as they are, the best stories rise and fall ephemerally upon the waters of time, which they neither choke nor obscure. They are like waves of time, full of the energy and substance of the water, making it into patterns to the delight of imagination. Hence, a good story starts and stops and includes somewhere a crest or climax, awesome in some stories, gentle in others. Hence also, a good story has rhythm. Its events (not to mention the phrases of its rhetoric) are connected in a round of time. These qualities a good story shares with poetry, music, and dance. I believe, indeed, that all the temporal arts, including narrative, are descended from dance, which is built upon our bodies' rhythms in time and space.

To get from dance to story we have to abandon nothing, but we have to add or emphasize something that is but latent in dance: the sense of a purposeful act undertaken by choice. Stories have characters, and what these choose to do engenders the story's plot. For instance, the parable of the good Samaritan is plotted according to the choices made by the priest, the Levite, and the Samaritan. We may look at plot either from the vantage point of the characters in it, in which case it appears as the "destiny that shapes [their] ends," or from the perspective of the author, in which case the plot is his or her design upon time. To plot is to contrive, and to contrive is to arrange an action toward a certain end by forethought. No story is spontaneous in the way a simple dance or song may be. All stories suggest a fall from pure grace or spontaneity.

In *Genesis* the fall has two stages. The first is God's decision to do something, to bring order to an earth he finds "without form." The second is the appearance in the garden of the fruit tree labeled, "Do not eat." Once the first stage has occurred, something like the second must follow. Or, to turn it around, if the second stage, which represents the morality of choice, is to be in the story, then the fall of God's creative act must formally precede it, since this is a story about the contrivance of the moral scene within which all other stories are enacted. *Genesis* 1 and 2 hook two creation stories somewhat awkwardly together to represent these two stages. So compelling is the logic that for many centuries people did not notice the patchwork although, once noticed, it is rather obvious. A creation myth is a story behind the story, and as soon as a god or any other agent structures a world the first "fall" has occurred. The message of every story is that the waters of life are troubled.

As if we didn't know. The story tells us *how* they are troubled, by what action, on what occasion, with what result and what feeling. In stories we read of tragic storms, lyrical eddies, epic meanderings, comic ripples, mythic currents, cataracts of farce or terror, and more. The world's literature is a great atlas of the waters of time, and the genres are its division into the familiar kinds of disturbance.

Without stories, as everyone knows, time would be monotonous. We tell stories not only to while away the time but also to shape it, render it meaningful, make it our own. Conrad's *Heart of Darkness* begins with men on a ship in calm water asking for a story to pass the time. Marlowe's tale is a cyclone upon that calm water. By its end, we have been taken not only into the heart of Africa but also to the eye of a dreadful storm. We may be horrified by the destruction of Kurtz, the leading character, but at least something has happened. The story has told time.

The hardest time to tell is my time. "Where did you go? Out. What did you do? Nothing." I know that I am fifty years old, but I have a hard time seeing my time.

In my year-long experiential course with students, the hardest yet most powerful part is when we try to tell our stories. People love to talk about themselves, but they do not know the shape of their time. Most (such is our white middle-class culture) will rely upon material exhumed in psychotherapy. Its virtue is that it is personal and has taken some pain to discover. Its fault is its blindness to the part played in all our stories by money, social class, tradition, and ideology. You would think, from most of the stories, that time flowed only through the nuclear family. People are aware of other realities, but they seem to locate them outside of time, where they also put the world of nature.

If I had more Black, especially poor Black, people in my class, it would be different. All oppressed people cultivate a livelier sense of story than those in the mainstream, and for good reason: to survive and get on they have to know the time of day.

The stories of women are getting better (usually better than the men's) as their consciousness about their place in society is raised. Now there is something to do. Now there is more knowledge about what has been done (the history of women), now there is greater sense of responsibility and with it the lure and fear of action. A few years ago my wife and I, during a workshop, requested small groups of women to invent stories in which the protagonist was a woman. There were twelve such groups in the room, and only one of them was able to come up with such a story. The others all fantasized romantic tragedies in which a woman started out as the central figure only to end up as the wife, mistress, queen, slave, or victim of a male hero. As I understand women's liberation, it is the attempt of women to become protagonists in their own stories.

By comparison with women, white men are usually very self-determined. They have been educated to take charge of their own lives. But they like to deny it. I read three motives in this. First, the Horatio Alger quality of their upbringing is increasingly contradicted by bureaucratic culture. Second, the self-determination a man *does* have, unless it be very great, is best preserved by camouflage. Third, if a man *is* responsible for himself in our society then he incurs guilt for its injustices. For these reasons, if not more, most men I know blur their stories. They obscure the major decisions they have made, almost as if there were none; and they tend to omit, by taking for granted, the time, place, and social class of their childhood. In my course a number of men have preferred to tell their stories as fantasies or allegories, suggesting a certain coyness. Christian teaching often compounds the problem by encouraging self-effacement, and by implying that the only story that matters is the one, big saga of the world's redemption.

To stimulate the students' narrative imagination, I have found one device of most help. I got it from my studies of the structure of stories in literature. I begin by asking the students to think at random about their present existence.

Next, I invite them to daydream about their future, making no distinction between what they think will happen and what they wish for. Then I ask them to go back in time to find the event with which their story begins. I announce that they may choose any event, anywhere, at any time except that they may not choose the moment of their birth or their conception in the womb. Then I wait to see what happens.

When I do this exercise, I entertain myself by watching the students' faces. I can tell when we start that some are puzzled or bored to reflect on their present existence. In the absence of directives about what to look for, they do not know what interests them, and they refuse the first images that come to mind (although in my opinion these are the most important) because they do not trust the spontaneous work of their imaginations, nor do they suppose that their feelings, which prompt these images, hold good clues to what is significant. If I wait, however, while nothing is said, I can see on faces that some figures and thoughts are asserting themselves, and then I go on. I learn later that some have anticipated my timing and have gone ahead by inner motivation to the future.

Daydreaming about the future is pleasant for most of my students, especially since they have permission to indulge in wish-fulfilling fantasy. In this episode expressions on faces become playful, except for a few who find the future threatening.

When we turn to the past to search for a beginning, the game becomes serious. Now persons' bodies become contorted. Eyes squint and mouths twist. Some persons display perplexity by tying fingers in knots or making fists. The task is not painful, however. Its obvious reward is going to be pleasurable—the achievement of a new purchase on time and self.

No person with whom I have ever done this exercise (and I have used it with groups outside of course as well) has failed to come up with a beginning, and for most it has been an event to which they had paid little attention before. I will not claim that lives are changed ever after, but I will say that the work adds a surprising amount to self-awareness and the "owning" of one's history. When I put myself through the sequence, I was astonished by the certainty with which it came to me that my life, as I know it, began with my decision at about the age of eight *not* to run away with the circus. The students laughed when I told them, for they experienced a comic recognition of me as theologian *qua* circus-master.

If you have the beginning of your story, engendered by a sense of where it is going or wants to go now, you have the whole. Here again is the loop of existential time.

Do we get, in this way, our true stories? Are we not still subject to self-deception, and do we not invent self-serving fictions? Something tells us we need an analyst, a priest, a prophet, a revelation to be able to know our stories as they really are.

The mystery now. The comedy. The absurd pretention, the valor and the loss.

Yes, the beginning I choose for my story is a function of my present-future existence. It will be no more authentic than I am now, and no less. If I am neurotic, self-serving, or in a posture of bad faith, the story I tell of myself will be the same and will tend to reinforce me as I am. I need thus the *critique* of my story by my neighbor, who may notice or remember what I am eager to forget. But most of all I need a summons, which may come through my neighbor, to responsible action in my present-future. Only this will enable me more truly to get at my story. As long as I evade the fullest ethical response to my present situation of which I am capable, as long as I choose in society to look the other way, my story will not come clean. It will rationalize my avoidance.

The story functions, then, not only with respect to my present and past but also in light of my future. Put simply, my story is not yet finished. Tomorrow, if I do not stagnate or barricade myself, I shall have a story different from today. Asked then to choose the beginning, I will posit some other point of origin. "In my end is my beginning."

So the stories fluctuate. To me, this is a sign of play and existential freedom. Nor would I want to worship a God who was forever stuck in one story. If I may be understood on the matter, I believe there is something of a rogue in God, the fellow who changes his story. Certainly in the Bible I find a God whose story changes, and I agree with Luther that not everything God said to Moses is also his Word to me now. This said, I recognize here a familiar, vexing puzzle about continuity and change in God.

Understood abstractly, change and continuity seem to be opposites. In any actual process of growth, however, continuity and change come together as two aspects of the same reality. To become a person, and to be a growing person, is to evolve stories about oneself in which continuity and change are integrated. When we speak of a person's identity, we do not mean only that in her which is ever the same. We are referring to her capacities of integration. A person who cannot put two and two together is said to be lacking in identity. Inability to correlate one's memories is loss of self-identity. The self is a capacity of organization, and organization is a mode of change. This applies to God as well as to creatures. Nothing is morally or intellectually wrong with changing a story unless we deny that we are doing so. One of the signs of a healthy person is precisely the ability to change one's story, to replot matters, and thus to rise to new occasions. This accounts for the value which religion places upon repentance and conversion.

The moral issue in all this has not to do with change as such nor identity as such but with who has the moral right to be the storyteller. In schools we learn more-or-less official sciences and histories. In religion, we learn that only God or gods know the real stories, which we must hear from priests, shamans, and sacred texts. In literature the task of the teacher and critic becomes, as Frank Kermode once remarked, that of establishing and maintaining a "cultural canon."

But what of my own story? I am back to the mystery, the absurd pretension, the valor and the loss. To whom shall I entrust my story if not to me? And who will be so fickle with it as I? Where is my friend Horatio on whom I may count to draw his breath in pain to tell my story?

"Tell him," pleads Vladimir to the boy messenger from the never-arriving Mr. Godot, "Tell him you saw me."

"I know," cried Job, "that my redeemer lives," although, like Mr. Godot, Job's savior figure did not put in an appearance.

"For God's sake, let us sit upon the ground and tell sad stories of the death of kings" (*Richard the Second*, III, ii, ll. 155–156).

> So we'll live,
> And pray, and sing, and tell old tales . . .
> As if we were God's spies.
>   (*King Lear*, V, ii, 1. 10–17)

And there were the easy riders crashing through the countryside and saying of it all, "We blew it."

Our stories, did you ask? As they really are? Go yourself and be God's spy.

The good stories float ephemerally on the waters of time, which they neither choke nor obscure.

All stories are fictions. A true story is as fictive as the rest, for without imagination the story does not arise. To be sure, some stories are lies, and some are so fanciful we pay them little attention. Those are the ones that choke and obscure the waters. The lie always wants to be believed, and fancy obscures by dazzlement. A true fiction does not ask for belief and does not seek to dazzle. It builds, if I may change my image, a house in time. Stories are the architecture of time. All buildings fall one day. Some last longer than others.

Now comes theology, like the bold coward, Saint Peter, walking upon the water. Saint Theology remembers that the prophets warned Israel about temples and holy places: "To your tents, O Israel!" Translated: "There are no buildings that can contain God or his law. There are no holy places, except maybe here or there from time to time when God stops Moses at a burning bush or Jacob wrestles all night somewhere with a heavenly stranger. But God moves on, so don't you settle down and fancy that your temples are the dwelling place of the wandering stranger God. Until his righteousness covers the earth as the waters cover the sea, he's never in one place long."

Saint Theology got a modern education, read these texts again, and said, "Good! The prophetic religion of Israel exalts time over space. Its God is not God of the land (that's naive Zionism and bad politics) but Lord of History. And history is the story of God's mighty acts from the beginning to the end. Ours is an *historical* religion, and I will tell everybody to walk with me on the waters of history, since we're all in the swim anyway."

"Watch out!" said the people in the pew—I mean, boat. "You'll sink!"

"Jesus will hold me up!" cried Saint Theology.

"You'd both better get in the boat!" they yelled back. So Jesus and St. Theology got in the boat, Saint Theology dripping and puffing like Peter of old.

"History's not very solid today," said somebody, while Saint Theology shivered and kept looking at the water.

When they got to shore (it was now about 1970) a few dragged out other boats and put to sea again, and most hauled their boat up to dry dock and wrote *Church* on it, but Saint Theology went off to read a book and think. None of them knew where Jesus was. Some thought he was ashore and some thought he had gone back on the water.

After a while, Saint Theology got an idea. "All our boats are stories," he said to himself. "We go to sea in history on these rafts. I read somewhere that stories float on the waters of time. Hey! Our ship, the Church, is a multistoried vessel. She floats on history because her hull is the spirit-filled story of God's incarnation in Jesus and how He will redeem all time, and all that. Jesus doesn't sink because he *is* the story. And I am alive today because I latched hold of the story. When I try to be logical and philosophical, I sink. But when I tell the old stories, and especially when I tell the big story, I stay afloat. Praise be to Jesus, the story-man!" And Saint Theology jumped up and ran off to tell everybody about the theology of story. "Get the ship out of dry dock!" he told them. "To your ships, O Israel! Down to the sea in ships! We will sail to the Kingdom on the waters of time!"

There were certain women at this time who began to mutter and shout. "The waters have always belonged to us," they said. "You men belong back on land playing with your Erector Sets. We are the ones that know about the wavy waters, and we don't get seasick as you do. Besides, your ship leaks, because you've got the story wrong and left all the women out." So they started to write the story over. Some wanted to leave Jesus out of it this time, which upset some others who couldn't figure out who the main character could be if it wasn't Jesus, but it didn't much matter because Jesus was still nowhere to be seen.

And there were certain Black people who screamed bloody murder. "Jeees-Us!" they yelled. "They've *all* got it *all* screwed up! The white men stole the story from us, and they whopper-jawed it to suit them, and they couldn't tell a good story if their life depended on it, and they are changing their story just when we are about to get a piece of the action." The Black people felt betrayed by Saint Theology, and they snarled at the women for not closing ranks with them against him.

Saint Theology paid little attention to these dissidents. "Always somebody rocking the boat," he said, and went off to a conference where he was chairman of the program committee.

At that time the Theology Society was trying to decide where to meet. Some said they should charter a cruise ship, but others thought better of it, so they met at the Hilton as usual. There they listened to Saint Theology on story. It sounded marvelous, so they agreed to meet next year at the Sheraton, along with the Literature Society, which was equally at sea.

What happened then is not clear. Some say that Poseidon caused an earthquake. "Put that in your anthology and smoke it," they report him as growling after the disaster. Others say that the place caught fire from the flaming tongues of ecstatic storytellers, and some say that Jesus (in other versions God) passed by and belched, leaving the Sheraton in shambles. It doesn't much matter, for they are all good stories, and time, as Puncher and Watson said, will tell.

Saint Theology escaped the fray and headed for church, where the hymns were louder than usual. "Eternal Father, strong to save," they bellowed, and the song went on to pray for "those in peril on the sea."

"Well," said Saint Theology, "the only thing I've learned

from all this is that the stories of time are no closer to God than the temples of space." And he went to sleep and dreamed he was a fish who swam in water without knowing it.

Our *true* stories, did you ask? Then tell me, from what holy place is God not to be moved?

The truth of God is no more confined to one story than to one location. Time has no advantage over space. They are equally mundane, equally spiritual. Take either away and we vanish. God will meet one person in space (this is your dancer and painter), another in time (this is your singer and storyteller), and neither without the other next. There is only one question: are we willing to form, and be responsible for, our own experiences in the world?

I say this is the only question, yet I say so in only one sense. The moral strength of God, in Christian tradition, is to have assumed responsibility toward the form of this world and toward Jesus as the human form of God. In other words, God authors God while forming Adam in the world, and does it again to form new Adam, new heaven and earth. The question posed to us is whether we will author ourselves by forming our world.

I have a friend who says: "Get clear about your source. Then *you* can be free to be *you*."

The good story asserts itself freely, knowing it floats upon water that flows, more freely yet, from a source at the head of the stream. The story of Jesus is not more true than the living water it tumbles, cruciform, into shape.

Human Experience
Is Word of God

My experiences follow one another ceaselessly, with near-infinite variety. Of what religious or moral significance can my experiences be when they are are plentiful as sands upon the shore?

I believe that the varied plenitude of our experiences provides the clue to their ethical and religious meaning. Briefly, it is this: the moral and religious life requires that we gather our myriad experiences into significant stories, until life acquires pattern. So also our countless primary experiences represent the encounter of life with life, making patterns where chaos was. We are engaged in the continual formation of our selves and our world.

This is the activity which Bible and theology have called the Word of God.

Few doctrines have split modern Christianity as deeply as that of the Word of God, a concept cherished by some and abhorred by others. In the main, it is cherished by those who have been willing to identify the Word of God with Scripture and preaching. It has been abhorred by those who refuse such an identification, fearing its literalistic and authoritarian consequences, yet not knowing what else to make of the concept. Except among fundamentalists, the doctrine of the Word of God has received little attention since the trumpet call on its behalf by Karl Barth.

The doctrine has two main roots in Christian history, one in the Old Testament, the other in Greek philosophy. The two roots join in the New Testament, especially in the famous and deeply influential prologue to the Gospel of John: "In the beginning was the Word, and the Word was with God, and the Word was God. . . . And the Word became flesh and dwelt among us, full of grace and truth (Jn 1:1, 14)." Strange language, familiar though it be.

The Old Testament has no thought of the Word of God becoming flesh. There the "Word of the Lord" is invariably a message, a mandate, or a power. It summons Jeremiah to prophecy, for instance, and tells him what to say. It also, according to one of the psalms, creates the heavens. In Genesis 1, a passage the author of the Fourth Gospel has in mind, light comes as soon as God opens his mouth. To this the Fourth Evangelist seems to add: "Yes, and an even more steady light shines when God appears in human form."

Since it is my purpose to show that human experience is revelatory of God, our co-creator, I am going to link arms with early Christian theology in its thought about the Word of God. In that theology the Greek term *logos*, the term used in John 1 and often translated "word," was very important. I must show that "word" is only one, and not the primary, meaning of that term. I must show that a *logos* is a pattern, a gestalt, an experience. Therefore, the "word" of God is an experience of God. This is what Karl Barth was tempted to say but came to believe he ought to deny. (See his *Church Dogmatics,* vol. 1 Part 1, esp. pp. 98–283.) A bad mistake, I'm sure.

As I said, *logos* is usually translated as "word." This it had come to mean long before the Old Testament was put into Greek and before the New Testament was written. Yet to equate *logos* with "word" is misleading, ever more so as time goes by.

I turn to G. F. Kittel's *Theological Dictionary of the New Testament*. There, almost in spite of the strong Word-theology of that compendium, I learn that *logos* stems from a root *legein* which originally meant to glean, gather, or collect. (Notice that it does not mean to talk.) At once I discern the basis of the early Christian doctrine of *logos* as creative principle, and also I perceive an affinity between *logos* and gestalt. A gestalt is a "structured, unified whole," a pattern of discernment, a shape arising from chaos. This is precisely what *logos* meant in the writings of Philo (the Hellenistic Jewish philosopher who so influenced the prologue to John) and in the early Christian theologians. A *logos* is a gestalt. The principle of *logos* will be the principle of patterning, recognition, creation and awareness. When *logos* comes later to mean "word," it will be with the sense that words are the names of what we gather up into wholes, what we recognize, have awareness of, and experience. If Jesus is called the *logos* of God (as in John 1), it means he is the form in which God recognizes (is most aware of) human being. In that case, Jesus also becomes the form in which human beings can best recognize God. The divine and the human meet in mutual recognition in the face (gestalt) of Jesus.

To these insights we must add the thought of power. In our culture one does not assume that recognition is power, but ancients knew better. They understood, as do primitive peoples, that to *see* something is to gain power, while also it is to acknowledge the power in what is seen. Hence, the Greek *logos*, like the Hebrew *dabar*, denoted both recognition and power. I shall make this point with a story.

Imagine we are no longer telling tales of exploits by firelight, are no longer Don Juans educating young Castanedas into the secrets of an animistic world, have ceased to be hunters imagining beforehand the chase of the sacred animal on the morrow. In all those cases we should want to convey awareness of structures and powers in the nonverbal world. "And then," we might say near the climax of our story, "I heard (or saw or felt) the *logos*!" In today's idiom: "And then, the thing happened!"

"What, Uncle?"

"The power of it! The Beauty! I trembled. But you have to be quick then, for it does not stay. I was once in the mountains for twelve days and saw the *logos* for only one instant."

"Will you take me there, Uncle?"

"If the *logos* calls me."

Imagine all this is no longer. We are agricultural people now, get our food from farmers (some of whom still talk strange), live in the town, and are attached to the king's household. What is the most important occurrence for which we must look out? The word of the king. As the man said after he had raised the offspring of a parrot mated with a tiger: "I don't know what it is, but when he talks I listen!" The *logos* has become the word of the powerful.

From the word of the king come all the tamed words of the court, the household, the civil servants, the school teachers, and the culture. All the *logoi* are domesticated in civilization. They are brought under the rule of the culture and (same thing) the rule of "reason." After a while people forget that there were *logoi* before there were languages, long before anyone thought to call a word a word. But the word for what wasn't a word survives and is tamed, now to refer only to what the schools of the culture know. All the dictionaries now say that *logos* means "word," and meanwhile the lion is still in the mountains.

By the roar of the Lord were the heavens made.
"Be quiet, God! You'll wake up the artists."
"R O A R ! !"
"Now you've done it! The theologians are waking up, too."
"Go back to sleep," said God, and decided to create the heavens some other way.

Bonaventura, the thirteenth-century Franciscan theologian, said that God created the "whole world in a single glance." I like that, as I like the thought of God's roaring, too.

Much is made in the literature to the effect of *logos* being "the rational principle." Fine, as long as we do not fancy that in order to be rational something needs to be verbal. Is the shape of a tree rational, or the feel of a baby's skin? Ratio, the root of "rational," means proportion: form, shape, pattern. Usually one hears that *logos* stands for whatever is intelligible. Fine again, as long as we do not suppose that whatever is intelligible can be understood. I think that the four last quartets of Beethoven are intelligible, but I do not understand them. The same goes for the colors of sky. It would be clearer if we said that *logos* stands for whatever is recognizable. Fundamentally a *logos* is not a sign, a symbol, or a unit of language. It is a dynamic form, perceived as such.

If *logos* did not mean something like this, it is difficult for me to see how the Fourth Gospel and the early theologians could have asserted that a *person*—not a book, a sermon, or a principle—was the *logos* of God. Surely they intended to say that in Jesus they perceived the dynamic, human face of God. They did not declare that this Gallilean had *spoken* the Word of God. They said plainly that the divine *logos* is what he *was*.

At the end of the first century A.D., Ignatius of Antioch called the Christ the Word of God "proceeding from silence."

I go back now to that verb, *legein*, from which the noun *logos* is descended. *Legein* will eventually lead to the Latin word *legere*: to read. Yet even in Latin the word retained some of its original meaning, which had nothing necessarily to do with reading or speaking. As I said above, the original sense was to glean, to gather, to collect. In other words, to put something together, to make a structured, unified whole. Such gathering up and forming is exactly what God does in both creation stories in Genesis.

With great wisdom (perhaps gained from observations of children) the Genesis authors depict God as naming what he structures. We get the impression that the naming is somehow part of the structuring (which may place these among our earliest texts in the sociology of knowledge). However, the naming does not of itself cause the structuring but instead completes it. The Word of God is neither some language coming out of his mouth to make things happen nor is it the names he gives to those things. Rather, it is the gleaning, gathering, and collecting by which he forms a heaven and earth he can recognize and say yes to.

With such a thought, I have made a translation of part of the prologue to John. I have wanted to get behind the cloud of familiarity that hangs over the Word of God. What follows is not a paraphrase but a translation, taking *logos* in its original sense:

At the start was the gathering up,
And the gleaning was toward God,
And God was the gathering up.

This gleaning at the start was
     toward God.
Through this, everything
     was born,

And apart from this, nothing
   was born at all.
In this gathering up was life,
And the life was the light that
   belongs to humanity,
And the light appeared in darkness,
And the darkness did not put it out.

      . . .

And the gathering up
   turned into human flesh
And encamped among us.
We saw the splendor of it,
Splendor like someone pure-born
   from the father,
Full of blessing and truth.

                —John 1:1–5, 14

We cannot intuit the creativity of God, nor sense its ethical meaning, unless we become aware of our own creativity in helping to gather up from chaos the very world in which we live. Although we may prefer not to think so, being quite ready to leave responsibility to God or to nature, we do continually form worlds, words, and patterns from the chaotic silence upon which we move like boats upon vast seas. As Sartre says, the images in our conscious minds are products of the "intention" we bring to life moment by moment. In my every beginning is my gathering up, my aim, my focus, my intention to have a world.

Christianity teaches that the creative ability to gather up form from chaos is a divine quality in the human being. It is a major part of what is called the "image of God" in humanity. Usually this quality is called "reason," but my investigations of *logos* and Scripture lead me to regard it as the capacity to gestalt the world, to create a human environment. This approach casts light, I think, upon some of our confusions about God.

One of the ways we religious people often confuse ourselves is to use the one name, God, for two quite different meanings, not stopping to notice that we cannot logically intend both at the same time. I hope to explain this by using the vocabulary of Gestalt psychology.

Two fundamental concepts in Gestalt psychology are "figure" and "ground." By "figure" is meant any discernible object, event, concept, or idea. That is, anything we can bring to focus. In other words, a gestalt.

"Ground" refers to the field or background from which the figure emerges, against which its contours are discerned, and into which the figure disappears as soon as our attention moves to some other, newly appearing figure. Ground and figure are in a reciprocal relation. Different as they are, the one implies the other. The relation is also dynamic: knowledge requires that our attention frequently shift, focusing and refocusing, continuously forming gestalts in relation to the infinite potential of our environmental ground.

Sometimes when we speak of God we intend a figure. At other times we imagine God as ground. We can never mean both at once.

A figure is always finite. Ground is infinite. The logical difficulty Christian theology always encounters is that God is both finite and infinite. This being illogical, it is usually described in paradoxes, as in the classical Trinitarian statements.

I suggest that theology stop trying to resolve a logical puzzle that is not at all puzzling in psychology. However, to bring ourselves and our theology to that point we will have to get over the notion that infinity is somehow better or more real than finitude. We would have to come to the psychological and existential insight that an ethical life requires equality of value for the infinite and for the finite. We would have to hold this to be the case not only for ourselves but also for God. That means giving up the attempt to think of God as one, and one only. Here I suppose I am at odds with classical theology as well as with the neoclassical Process theologians since Alfred North Whitehead. I'll come in a moment to the doctrine of the Trinity, the classical answer to the question I am raising.

As figure, God is person. I will say that more boldly: as figure, God is *a* person. Tillich and Aquinas would both be horrified. For them, the article before the noun renders it finite. The finite images of God—*a* person, *the* Father, etc.—are symbols or analogies in the eyes of most classical theolgians, who desire never to allow an image of God to be taken for the reality of God. In his transcendent essence, God is beyond all our images and finite figurations. Therefore, God is not *a* person, although he is imagined as such. In formal construction, theology may then say that God is person, which means person*al* or person*hood,* but not *a* person.

How I have changed on this point! I have studied

philosophy well. I was educated in the history of literary interpretation, know the traditions of symbolic and analogous reasonings, can recognize a metaphor when I see one. I used to be scornful of all who take figures of speech literally. Theology was for me a symbol-system, and the good theologian kept readers aware of it. The Bible, too, was a symbolic literature; and its religion was, as Tillich said, a "search for ultimate reality." Never confuse the symbol with what it symbolizes.

More than to any other one person, I will give John Heider credit for my turn. He was a group leader at Esalen, and I was a member of a group he was getting started. After an hour or so, he said to us: "I know nothing about you except what I see and hear in this room, and I take it literally."

I was dumbfounded. The man was as intelligent as anyone I had met in a long time. His tact with people was superb. He had certainly thought about the statement he made. How could he not realize that in order to know us he had to interpret, to read our behaviors as signs or symbols of what we really were?

Not until later did I read Perls and Goodman on Gestalt therapy's working "at the uppermost surface." So I was stunned. Gradually, however, some forgotten bits of learning came back to mind to help me appreciate what Heider was getting at. I list them:

1. A piece by John Ciardi years ago in the *Saturday Review* telling of a woman who wrote asking what he meant when he said in a poem that Degas

Kept an old Rembrandt by his bed
To hang his pants on.

Ciardi replied that he meant that the painter Degas had kept an old painting by Rembrandt in a frame propped up near his bed so that when he retired he could hang his trousers on it.

2. Protests of many writers, Ciardi being only one, against too much "deep reading" of their works in schools.

3. Aristotle: "It is by their actions that we know what men are."

4. Sartre: "Existence precedes essence." "You are what you do."

5. Jesus: "By their fruits you shall know them."

6. Susan Sontag: *Against Interpretation*.

7. A poem by a friend of mine saying,

   "The painter's eye is to be believed."

8. Tillich and Giotto's trees. When a student, I heard Tillich lecture on Giotto. Using slides, he pointed to the trees and informed us that Giotto had painted not trees but "treehood." I looked at the tiny straight trunks with balls of green on top and decided Tillich was profound. I wrote "treehood" in my notes. The next year I went to Italy. Arriving in Tuscany, I broke out laughing. There, growing everywhere, were perfect specimens of Giotto's "treehood!" Whatever philosophy Giotto had, he also had 20/20 vision.

9. Bertolt Brecht: *"Die Warheit ist konkret."*

I had been taught, or at least thought I had, that to say the truth is concrete would land one in positivism. Metaphoric thinking in philosophy, art, and religion was your great protection against a positivistic reduction of the world to two dimensions and against the banalities of Biblical literalism. I was still a Platonist, and full of nonsense about the Incarnation.

Augustine, of all people, was of help in my transition. Expounding what became the standard medieval "fourfold levels of interpretation," he had said of the first, or literal, level: "First get it straight that it means what it says before you go on to the other levels." I do not share Augustine's assumption that everything in the Bible is true and authoritative, but I think he was right to say that its statements should be taken literally. Even if we go on, as I often do, to find metaphoric senses, the bedrock of every good metaphor or symbol is the literal observation (the figure) on which it is based.

In my thought today the literal *is* the figurative. I am not entering here into the sort of questions historical criticism raises—for instance, to ask of certain events described in the Bible whether they really happened. Such questions are important for our contextual sense when reading but they are never decisive for the meaning of a passage. What is decisive is the figure itself—the event described, the image evoked, the syntax of the sentence. This figure, whatever it be, acquires meaning in relation to context: the context provided by the Bible itself (or part of it) and the reader's own sense of global context. The figure itself, however, is the bearer of the meaning. It may not be reduced to its context without fading into the "ground." It may not be interpreted into some meaning other than itself without violation to the text in which it occurs.

The reciprocal relation between image and context, or between figure and ground, helps me to understand the confusion in much of our talk about God. Some of the time, though not always, we mean by "God" a figure. As figure God is manifest in particular, focused, finite ways. He is a *persona,* a character in stories.[1] As figure, God walks in the garden in the cool of evening, tells Abraham to get out of Ur, meets Moses on a mountaintop. Moses got mad. God turned his back, would not show his face. The figure is one of the more vivid in the whole Old Testament. As figure, God speaks to Jeremiah and appears to Isaiah in the temple "high and lifted up."

In the New Testament, God appears as figure in Jesus of Nazareth. This gives me the approach I would take to the doctrine of Incarnation today: Jesus is the historical figure of God *non pareil.* Hence, the figural approach to biblical interpretation in the Middle Ages is not as far wrong as its present-day reputation suggests. What *was* wrong was its use in an antihistorical, analogical frame of reference. Understood in a Gestaltist way, however, figural understand-

---

[1] I am aware that *persona* is a word derived from the theater and means "mask." Strictly speaking, it means a mouthpiece, for the masks worn by Greek and Roman actors were so made as to amplify the sound of the voices. I point out that the basic use of masks in theater and primitive religious ceremony is not to conceal but to reveal. The mask is the figure of the god, the sacred animal, the character (this word also means "figure") and so on. The use of a mask to conceal is derivative. The story of how that use came into theater is not unrelated to the theological and philosophical motifs I am discussing, but I leave it now aside.

ing affirms what is historical and literal: *Die Wahrheit ist konkret*.

I apologize to the shade of Brecht for using his quote in a Christian context, which no doubt offends him. But *he* got the quote from Hegel and took it out of Hegel's context. My use of it differs from both. Unlike Brecht, I do not think the idea is antireligious. Unlike Hegel, I do not think that Truth or Absolute Spirit *becomes* concrete. Truth *is* concrete from the moment we can talk or think about it. When the spirit hovers over the waters, it is not yet truth, or anything else. The minute I ask, "Well, what is it, and why do I write sentences like that?" I know that such truth as may be in my thought is already "figured."

Sometimes by "God" we mean not "figure" but "ground," which is why theology has often adopted a *via negativa*. The ground of a figure has no definition or character. It is what is *not* figured. It is that field *against* which the figure shines, the water *from* which the wave arises, the depth *into* which the figure disappears. It is the *all,* and without the figure it is *nothing,* chaos.

Our language about the divine ground is shot through with negation and with terms that are purely relational. The ground is (theoretically) the relation of all relations, which is literal nonsense. When we refer to God as ground we do not know what we are talking about.

To think of God as infinite ground is not new. Tillich sometimes called God the "ground of Being," which I would change to "the ground of the figure." Like Socrates, theology has almost always known that both revelation and reason bring us to the shore of ignorance, or mystery. All wisdom knows this, and I do not for a moment contradict or denigrate the traditions of West and East that lead us to that shore and bid us be silent before it. My concern is not the foolish one of trying to figure out the ground. My concern is to ground the figure.

My quarrel is with those who assume or conclude that a figure is less than its ground. Far from grounding a figure, this dissolves it. By the same token, such an assumption severs "ground" from its true reciprocity with figure and leaves us conceptually without anything at all. When a figure is understood somehow to be less than its ground, figure becomes "figure of speech." What is concrete becomes opaque. What is plain becomes mystery. What is finite becomes inferior to infinity. All limit becomes somehow wrong, bad, less than what *really* is. The metaphoric becomes the picturesque. In general, life becomes stand-in for something else. God knows what. I say, God doesn't.

Sometimes, as I have said, we mean by God a figure, sometimes we mean an infinite ground, and we never mean both at once. This suggests a duality. Shall we say the dualism belongs only to our limited, finite minds, or shall we say the duality is also in God?

Were I to decide to identify God with some unity imagined as the prior condition of all experience, I would pay the price classically paid: a consequent denigration of experience. At every level, philosophical and practical, God is experienced inconsistently. Shall we then say that experience lies? Does God contrive experience so that it will not reflect the unity of God? And what shall we say about the drive toward unity that is so much a part of our intellectual and moral life?

The latter question holds the clue. Our experienced quest for unity is exactly what it seems like—a quest. The same, I believe, is true for God. Like us, God is divided and aims to become whole. Integrity is an achievement. Its first moment is the one I have called "hesitancy" in my picture of God in self-deliberation on the day before creation (chapter 4). Integrity's final moment is eschatalogical, that fulfillment of which we have promise but not guarantee.

Some theologies, Manichaeism especially, have been clearly dualistic. I assert, along with Manichaeism, that the divine and human drama is real. That old heresy saw the script as one in which a good God had to vanquish or outwit an evil God. In other words, the duality of God was seen in terms of good *versus* evil. I see it otherwise. To me, the duality is between finite and infinite, both of which are good.

From this vantage point, evil is the result of not giving equal value to both finite and infinite. (Can a person serve two masters? Yes, if neither is evil.) The good heart is one which, seeing the tension between finite and infinite, moves into it courageously, knowing neither how to overcome it nor to avoid it with integrity. The evil heart chooses one over the other.

If I am on the right track, then the theology of the church, unlike the behavior of Jesus, has for the most part been wrong. Christian theology has characteristically devalued finite experience in favor of the infinity of God. The moral consequences have been disastrous. The finitude of God, testified to in the doctrine of Incarnation, has been locked up under a once-for-all seal so tight that the creativity of God has become a dead issue. Once in a while there comes along a Gerard Manley Hopkins to break the seal, as he did in his vision of "inscape," but theology will not follow. Hopkins gave up poetry and surrendered to theology. His "inscape" was partly the fruit of the medieval theologian, John Duns Scotus, but theology did not follow him, either. Scotus had affirmed too much finitude in the mind of God to suit the Church's love of infinity.

The Church is very aware of the sin of idolatry, which is the exaltation of a finite thing into the place of the infinite. The church is less aware (almost oblivious) of an idolatry of the infinite, as if creation somehow sullied God. Tillich saw the problem and then promptly excused God from involvement. In this he was typical, although his formula is unorthodox. He identified the Fall with creation (which is unorthodox), but he also held that the God of creation is not the ultimate God, whom he called the "God beyond God." This is simply to transfer the problem. In the last anyalsis both Tillich and the more orthodox keep God pure by making history a grand mistake.

The church seems to protect God from finitude as a parent might protect a child from contamination by its own mess. Purity becomes an absolute virtue. Many modern theologians, especially those concerned with ethics and liberation, have tried to praise the dirty hands that all ethical action requires, but this is in vain as long as God is kept above it all in the purity of infinite Oneness.

Purity of the one God is often defended by doctrines of transcendence. I resist a long tradition that imagines transcendence spatially and thus removes it from the domain of action. The key terms in its explication are usually words like *limit*, *beyond*, *over against*, *above*, *outside of*, and so on. Such images are perhaps natural enough, but I think they find their philosophical support in ontologies of substance inherited mainly from Plato. If such conceptuality were carried into my duality between finite and infinite, it would suggest that transcendence applies to the infinite God and not the finite God. This would be as bad anthropologically as it would be theologically; for it would mean that finite humans lack transcendence, or that we have it in some other kind than God. Denigration of our experience has followed from such ideas.

In my view, transcendence has no particular connection with spatial limit, although space is not to be eliminated from any concept and although I am aware that *transcendence* literally means "movement across." I therefore ask: across what? And I answer: across the moment of hesitance between the potential ground and the actual figure. Transcendence is existential. It has to do with freedom, intentionality, and choice. It is as finite as it is infinite. It is preeminently felt in what I called earlier "the good heart" moving courageously into the tension between finite and infinite. A moment of transcendence is a moment of courageous freedom and creativity, and from this its ethical and theological importance comes.

I express this matter succinctly by saying that transcendence is choice. To transcend is to choose. But a choice cannot be made unless one is *in* a situation. Therefore, transcendence requires immanence, with which it is, as I shall show in a moment, identical. We should not think of the opposite of transcendence as immanence but rather inaction or removal from the scene.

Transcendence is not the same as the moment of hesitance but is the movement across or through it. If no action is reached, there is no transcendence. In the measure in which a figure is blurred or an action irresolute, transcendence is diminished.

Transcendence, then, is not a capacity, a potentiality, or any inherent quality. The word should not be used to refer to anything that *is* or *may be* but to something that does or does not happen. The noun is misleading, and to ask whether one does or does not believe in the transcendence of God verges on the foolish. A good reply would be, "Let's look and see what God does next."

To choose or to act is to transcend. The act *is* the quality and has no reality except in the moment of the action. Introspection reveals that a mere *capacity* for choice, a being poised at the edge of choice, or existing in its sheer potentiality neither seems nor feels like transcendence. It comes across as immaturity or dread. To be stuck in the moment of hesitance is to experience loss of transcendence.

In the Old Testament the transcendence of God is apparent above all in the act of creation—"Let there be"—and in the choice of Israel as covenant partner. Both are commitments to finitude, while at the same time both are undertakings of infinite risk. The motif becomes even clearer in the New Testament with God's infinite commitment to the finitude of Jesus. The transcendence of God evokes the transcendence of Israel by way of the prophetic command to choose Yahweh and not the other deities. This is paralleled in the New Testament by Jesus' rejection of the temptations in the wilderness.

It is hopeless to look to the horizon, the ground, or to

infinity to find transcendence. Rather, we must look to the center, where we will find the figure and the act of choice that brings it, momentarily, to be. All organisms transcend their environment precisely by their immersion in it—that is, to the degree that they *act* in it. Their acting is a measure of their engagement. If the human environment is vaster and more complex than that of an orange tree, it means that the human is more deeply engaged *with* the environment— by virtue of eyes, ears, ambulating limbs, and so on, including imagination. Far from being free *of* of the environment, humans are free in it, to it, and with it, provided only that they recognize how they and their environment coinhere. Awareness of this seems to me the authentic motive for scientific inquiry. The motive is falsified when it is forgotten that every increase of power gained through knowledge entails a corresponding increment of responsibility to the environment, a growth in choice (that is, transcendence) and ever deeper divine/demonic encounter.

Divine transcendence, I reason, is not to be looked for in separation from the world, but rather engagement with it. Transcendence is radical immanence. I suppose this is the heresy of panentheism. Once one starts on the road of immanence, it is better to go all the way. Christianity especially needs to do this. Otherwise, the immanence of God in the incarnate Christ becomes such a sheer paradox as to be robbed of a comprehensible motive. The only way to explain it then is to picture it as a divine condescension (*kenosis*) in the name of love. But this is psychologically vicious.

The psychological damage done by the Christian myth of a pure (because purely other) God who condescends to humankind in the name of love without getting his essence dirty (immaculate conception, creation without encounter) seems to me horrifying. It breeds either self-contempt or the arrogance of purity. The Church has fabricated a myth of a God who is self-sufficient yet loving. This myth makes the church schizophrenic.

The definition of transcendence as otherness or beyond-ness, sometimes in mild logical manner (as, for instance, in Gordon Kaufmann's essays) and sometimes by strident assertion (as in Barth), has the result of making theology very skittish about experience.

I hold experiences to be occasions and sources of revelation, as they are also occasions and sources of knowledge. Revelation is *gnosis*, provided we do not imagine *gnosis*, after the fashion of its corrupters, to be secret doctrine but rather awareness of spiritual presence in dynamic forms. Such wisdom is incommunicable except by participation. All revelation is primary. Would only that Brunner had said so, instead of dragging in a "secondary" category for Barth (wrongly) to attack! Not all revelation, however, is of equal importance, no more than do all our experiences have the same value. Their importance depends on the function they come to have in the more or less integrated gestalts we make of our lives.

I do not mean only that we continue to collect, by experience, footnotes to the revelation in Christ. The claim that the Christian revelation is "once-for-all" is hyperbole. It is testimony of God's infinite commitment to finitude. From it, however, we may not conclude that Jesus is the norm for all time, nor that God may not make such a commitment in *another* form.

We do continually revise the form of the Christ according to experiences we choose, transcendently, not to deny. For instance: Are we to marry in Christ-like conscience? Is Jesus Black? Is the Christ necessarily male? Is God? Does the once-for-all character of the revelation in Christ obtain if we find quite alien forms of life in outer space? May the church change its mind on matters of essential doctrine? May women be authentically ordained?

I suppose the general tendency is to field such questions as these by saying that we modify our opinions in light of experience, while God remains the same. I do not think so. The conclusion I reach is that God does not remain the same. Not even essentially. God changes, as does all else that lives. All things change; some change faster than others. Even that maxim may change, but I have not noticed it doing so yet. As God changes, so does revelation. Far from being fixed (a sign of addiction) revelation moves. If there is any revelation at all, it changes.

The only way I can know the change, know revelation, is to attend to my experiences, including memory and hope. I must do this without reserve, although I still have to exercise judgement, which judgment is choice and transcendence.

Such being the case, I come to a declaration of faith: *all* my experience is Word of God for me. I mean the dirt, the pain, the confusion, the courage, the flinching, the growth, the dying, the hope, the despair, the church, the brothel, the he, the she, the dark, the light, the yes, the no, the pattern, and the mess. I mean the liberation *and* the prison. I mean the heroin no less than the poppy in the field: if I do not mean that, I do not mean the Cross as I mean the lilies of the field.

God, that hurts! *All* my experience is Word of God for me. Will I say that when King Heroin eats my child? Ask me when it happens. Ask the needle.

To love is to desire to touch. Love, like hatred, is an aggressive emotion. It moves *toward* its object and not away. The opposites of love and hate are fear and loathing. Perfect love, it is written, casts out fear.

Insofar as love is a spiritual state, its opposite is sin or alienation. I define sin as alienation, whether from God, from the neighbor, or from self. To feel alienated is to feel distanced, cut off, alone. For this reason, sin is self-willed, while love and grace bring the soul into harmony with the dance of heaven.

Whatever is untouchable is not an object of our love. Hence, the great ethical breakthroughs of the Christian religion of love, when they have from time to time appeared, have been to break down some social, political, religious, and psychological barriers that formerly protected the righteous from the unrighteous. This is the sense of St. Paul's controversy with the "Judaizers" in the early Church, and of St. Peter's dream of the sheet lowered from heaven full of unclean animals.

In the Gospels almost nothing is more characteristic of Jesus than his open attitude toward the poor, the weak, the sick and the despised. He eats with sinners, includes prostitutes in his fellowship, goes home with tax collectors, bends sacred law to human need, and displays an unprecedented spirit of equality toward women. His spiritual antagonists, as reported many times in the Gospels, are the Pharisees, because their religious attitude is that of purity, superiority, and exclusion. The story of the cosmic Christ (the anointed one of God) is built on a similar motif. From his birth in a stable, through his carpenter's training, his baptism at the hands of John, his ministry among the poor, and his arrest by political authorities, this savior figure is anything but set apart. The story climaxes with his entry into the realm no immortal was supposed to touch or be touched by—death and burial. The New Testament myth of the cosmic Christ, as William Blake saw, is of an embrace between the divine and the human. This motif it shares with many Greek and other pagan myths, the difference being that the union is no mere adventure but the expression of the heart and mind of God.

Whenever the Christian mission, in spite of all its horrors, displays a character we recognize as authentic, it serves to eliminate or weaken barriers of alienation among people. As far as human behavior is concerned, the good news of the gospel is that all are welcome to sit at the same table. Politically, this may be translated into democracy and liberation. Fundamentally the name for it is love.

The desire to touch, which is love, is not confined to the touching of persons. A child learns to see by touching all objects within reach, and the love of life there displayed may be retained or lost as we mature. To seek to touch, to learn from that, to receive and give in touching is a literal metaphor of healthy life. To be "in touch" is to be genuinely alive, while to be "out of touch" is to be dying.

When I say that love is the desire to touch, I may equally well say that love is desire for experience. All other desires have some different end in view. Lust, for example, is the desire for pleasure, to which end it preconceives experiences. Lust, not love, is blind. Desires for power, money, status, control, even beauty, all predetermine experiences in order to achieve an end to which the experiences are but instrumental. In my view, the Christian religion has often (most often) betrayed itself by subordinating experience to the "higher" aims of salvation and obedience. Indeed, I find in churches very often a deep suspicion of experience, as if life were bound to lead one into error and has to be tolerated out of necessity.

All desires except love prejudge experience and find something better by which to measure it. But love, as Paul said, "suffers long and is kind." Undeniably, there is something antinomian about love. This is because love is open toward experience and delights in it for its own sake. It has no standards except full receptivity toward the experience's full form. That is why there is something sacrificial about love, and why ancient marriage vows offered constancy "for better or for worse." The intent of marraige (as against other kinds of partnership) is to have the experience, no matter what it is. To be sure, this requires foregoing many *other* experiences; but love does not aspire to have everything, only to having fully (therefore giving fully to) whatever it does have. Love asks no reward that is not in experience itself. Hence, not even pain defeats love, although the fear and avoidance of pain will cripple love and bind it into law.

Breathe in Me, Breath of God

I BURN constantly. That holy fire the saints speak of is fueled continually in my body. It does not go out even when I sleep. On cool nights I lie close to my lover, that our fires may warm each other.

In all the vast distances of space, life and light appear as centers of fire, some far apart like remote suns, some clustered together like birds in a nest. The God who saves me from the last fire is the same who fired me into life at the meeting of two cells and has not ceased, since then, to kindle me.

The energy of God enters me through all my receptors. Nothing else does enter me except the energy of God. "Nothing," said Jesus, "that goes into a man can defile him." But since so much does go in, and since my appetite for it is so great, the name for this food is grace. I give that name even to bitter herbs, bad air, and poison. Even cigarettes. Although I know they are "hazardous to my health" and although I wish I had never acquired their habit, the smoke enters me as part of the grace of God. This does not seem to make good sense, yet I think it anyway, not for logic but for love of life. Grace, I reason, can be dangerous, or ugly, or painful, or destructive.

What if the very last fire, which some call Hell, is the same as this fire burning now, this incandescence of the lit universe, this radiance of consumption, aflame in agony on 125th Street and burning, too, in the green cyprus beside the blue Pacific? What if I am burning now for all the sins of my life stretching back to the Garden of Eden or to those primeval crimes by which my ancestors wreaked culture and civilization upon the suffering earth? Is there, can there be, a Hell more awesome than this present one where everything feeds off everything else and nothing lives but by death? Or, turning the image around to its more familiar form, do the flames of Hell have no beauty? In order to ask that question, which sounds as if it might have come from the lips of a John Calvin or a Jonathan Edwards, I must have either a heart of ice or a soul that knows itself already on fire. Robert Frost: "Some say the world will end by fire/And some by ice." And there was old Dante Alleghieri, finding at the center pit of Hell a body of ice, then climbing down its side until everything changed direction and he, by going downward, found himself ascending into the warm celestial light. What did Betty Fuller say the other morning? "I am convinced that the purpose of gravity is so that we can fly."

The paradoxes of poets are not baubles of fancy. They are the way imagination, which is the light of the mind, participates in the transformations we see with our eyes in the great fire roaring about us, those moultings and wave-breakings that Wallace Stevens called "the metaphysical changes that occur/Merely in living where and how we live." He said of these "metaphysical changes" that they are swarming in the mid-day air.[1]

I do not know what those suns we call stars eat. I have not read up on the combustions in the sky. I only know that down here, or over here, or wherever it is that we are in the pleroma of space, creatures like me burn by food and oxygen. I stare at the green plants because they are my sustenance. As the Psalmist lifted up his eyes to the hills, so I turn mine to the leafy green things. I used to think that my instinctive love of them was purely esthetic, until I learned that without them I should never have come to exist on this planet. Green forms feed my eyes, my soul, my stomach, and my lungs.

Not only can I eat many of the green plants, and not only do the animals I eat eat them, but also they supply to the air the oxygen I use to burn the food in my blood. If I did not know this, I would burn anyway. Knowing it, my mind is on fire. With knowledge, I burn my own burning. Sometimes I need water lest I scorch myself. I am the Samaritan woman at the well drawing one kind of water and getting two, one to bathe the cells of my body (which long for the sea they came from eons ago) and one to bathe the dry heat of my burning in the knowledge of good and evil.

A fire lives by oxidation of combustibles, and I live by burning the food I eat. The difference, of course, is that a fire

[1] "Esthetique du Mal," in *The Collected Poems of Wallace Stevens* (New York: Alfred A. Knopf, 1955), p. 326.

leaves only a heap of ashes while the food I burn builds up the form of a human being. Yet I, too, shall "return to dust" when my fire goes out. Like the fire, my truth is not in my flickering form alone but even more in my function. I am an energy transformer. As such, I take matter into my being that I may transform it and deliver it forth again. The hymn, echoing the parable of the talents, says, "We give thee but thine own." But woe to that steward who hoards without transforming the gift given.

The first thing I must do with a gift given or a bite taken is to make it my own. Aristotle said that "food is the unlike that can become like." The philosopher had a way of saying what is familiar, even obvious, in strange ways. Food is the familiar made strange, while digestion is the strange made familiar. To assimilate simply means "to make alike." The gift given, the food available must appear to me first as strange. If not, I cannot savor it, and half its value is gone. Then I must decide to incorporate this strange, to make it my own by destroying its present form for the sake of the energy it may become.

Taste is the censor, telling the muscles that chew and swallow whether to proceed or to go in reverse and spit. And taste, if the signals are go, is also the first step in digestion, for it tells my awareness how to assimilate any particular experience of eating. Taste *is* the digestive process insofar as it pertains to sensory awareness, while the rest of the process puts into my blood the combustibles that are going to be burned with the aid of oxygen.

When Kelly died, I learned about the food of the brain. In her, the light of imagination and awareness went out as soon as her brain did not get enough food. She fell into a diabetic coma. The first injury was to the cortex, and she never regained consciousness. The lower brain and the vegetative system it controls kept on going for several weeks. Then, for what reason I don't know, they also stopped. Kelly's fire went out by stages.

The brain, which is at once the most sophisticated and the most primitive organ of our bodies, uses two, and only two, substances for nourishment: sugar and oxygen. I try to imagine a being so rarified that it would consume only sugar and oxygen. I remember the Greeks saying that the one food of the gods is nectar. Only a god or a spirit, I fancy, would ask for no protein, no roughage, no variety but would all the time sip honey. Or only an infant perhaps, or maybe some creature at the dawn of evolution, some original stirring cell of life that had discovered how to adapt and keep itself going, how to take in and give out by the ingestion of something; and that something was sugar. In fact, there is such a creature among us still—the yeast in my kitchen. I do not even need to buy it in the store. If I set a mixture of sugar and water in a bowl on the window sill, it will in a few days pick up yeast cells from the air.

If, as I imagine, the cells of my brain, which is the crown of my consciousness, are the purest survival in me of the most primitive kind of life from which I am descended, then the song I thought wistful is true: I "make my livin' in candyland." I have done so from the beginning. This hell is heaven, and the Blakean dream of the marriage of heaven and hell is but the imaginative version of what is already the case, as the old printer well knew.

All the contemplative religions, including Christianity

and Judaism on their contemplative side, offer to the hungry an invitation at once simple and sophisticated as the brain: "O taste and see!"

Whoever accepts that invitation wakes up in the holy fire. When I do so, my body becomes a bellows, pumping air to the furnace that purifies, destroys, and makes new. I, who am a perfect shit, am one of the "sages standing in God's holy fire." The light within and around me is even more brilliant than the gold in Byzantine mosaics.

Nothing burns but by oxygen. Oxygen is the spirit of the fire, for lack of which the fire goes out. This substance, which is not the fuel but that which quickens the dead or dying fuel into new life, is not, in usable form, native to the air of our planet. It has come, and still comes, to the atmosphere by cooperation between green leaves and the light of the sun.

The earliest plants are the wild grasses. The flowering plants and the trees came later. The roots of the plants probe the earth for mineral food, while the leaves reach skyward for sunlight, magic substance of no weight, alchemical agent transforming the dross of earth into verdure. Ages before the first myth of the marriage of earth and sky, the green plants wedded them root and branch.

The green chlorophyl of the grass blade "digests" the plant's food, using sunlight and carbon dioxide. The by-product of this odd combustion is pure oxygen, which the plant exhales, furnishing the air, little by little, with enough to support animal life. Only after this miracle had worked for eons did there appear the first animal cell to live by burning sugar.

I live by inhalation, breathing in and breathing out. From the air coming in, I take the oxygen I require. Exhaling, I return the rest, plus carbon dioxide for the green plants. Also, sometimes I return the air in newly patterned form. Having nothing else to do, I tremble the air into waves of vocal sound. When I am finely turned, I give back the air as word and music. My fire crackles. The universe answers, for my word does not return to me void.

I am a word answering the word of God. Or, if you like, I am the word of God answering itself, returning not void but full.

To say "I am" is to say "I breathe." The verb *am*, some think, comes from a Sanskrit root meaning "to breathe." The Greek word for breath is *psyche*, which came also to mean soul and mind. *Pneuma*, the Greek word for spirit, means "air." So does the Hebrew *ruach*, which also means "wind." The German *Geist* is cognate with "gust." The French *l'esprit*, like the English "spirit," is from the Latin *spiro*, "I breathe." To inspire is to breathe into, while a conspiracy is a breathing with. My respiration is my constant re-breathing.

When I was in the womb, I had no need of my lungs. Suspended in amniotic fluid, I received oxygen from my mother's blood by way of the placenta. At about five o'clock in the afternoon on Sunday, May 31, 1925, I was expelled from my mother's womb into the surrounding air. My heart was pumping blood to my brain. The blood carried, among other things, sugar and oxygen. The sugar content was good for several hours, the oxygen for only a few minutes. My brain needs constant feeding. To live, I had to do something I had not done before: inflate my folded lungs by taking a gasp of air.

I do not know how they induced me to breathe. Some babies require no sharp stimulus. Others seem to. A familiar routine in our culture has been to hold the baby aloft by the feet and whack it on the back. This is cruel grace, usually unnecessary. To slap the baby is to say, "Breathe, God damn it!" The baby usually obeys. It is perhaps the first time in our lives we are commanded to do by law what we would otherwise do by love. How odd that our "Christian" culture should never have learned that law and grace move to the same end and therefore we could, if we would, arrive at grace by graceful means instead of flogging each other there, except that grace not trusted requires law to do awkwardly and painfully what love might do with a kiss. The midwife who slaps the baby is, I imagine, holding her own breath. So also the obstetricians, those mostly male midwives in our hospitals who come equipped with instruments of torture. Breathe in me, breath of God.

The baby, for its part, comes equipped with what it needs to start breathing; and the lack of oxygen as soon as the placenta separates supplies the motive, or, as I shall say in a moment, the condition *for* the motive. Inside the chest, folded, made ready, never used, are the two lungs. On the outside of the body is the skin. This surface is like a third lung and functions so throughout life, a membrane through which part of the oxygen we use transpires. Truth to tell, the interior lungs are an extension and specialized portion of the skin. Like the sensory organs (ears, nose, palate), the lungs develop in embryo from the epidermis, most of which becomes skin. The lungs retain some of their skinlike capacity to respond to touch. That is why many of us smoke—to experience a new sensation in the lungs, even though the smoke contains poison.

If you touch any part of a baby, the whole of it is likely to respond. We are born integrated. Life is a process of becoming, ever and again, disintegrated so that, if all goes well, we may reintegrate in a new way.

If you touch the skin of a newborn child, the whole of it responds, including certain muscles of the torso which, by contracting, open the chest and suck in some air. Moreover, there is a special reflex link between breathing and the sensory nerves in the skin. For this reason, *any* definite sensation felt by the skin of the newborn will stimulate the first gasp of air. It need not be brutal. A deliberate, deep caressing will do. So will immersion in water to present the skin with change in temperature—for instance, a brutal dip into cold water (think how we gasp when we step under a cold shower) or a more kind immersion into water rather warm.

Although I feel that the slam-bang way of inducing a baby to breathe is like law where gospel would better do, I understand the anxiety in the delivery room. The baby will die if it does not breathe, and it has but a few moments to start. The sucking action of the mouth, required for nursing, has been rehearsed *in utero*. Besides, there is no big hurry about eating. But if the oxygen supply is interrupted more than a very few minutes the brain will be permanently damaged, or the child may die. This is no time to stand on one foot. The baby must breathe.

"And he breathed into him the breath of life."

I must inquire into the Hebrew text. I wonder about that term *breath*. In the Hebrew, is it a noun or a verb? If it is a noun, how close is it to a verb? My instinct tells me the sentence should read: "And he breathed into him the breathing of life."

Be that as it may, I must not suppose that breath is a thing, a something, a substance. It is an action, a response, a doing, wherein I assume responsibility for myself. The first step in walking the lonesome valley ("Oh, nobody else can walk it for you") is to breathe.

By what miracle, by what *what*, is life transferred across the sparking gap between the living and the yet-to-live? Wake up, Adam, wake up. Come forth, Lazarus. Arise, my love. Master, he cannot hear you, for he is dead. Can these bones live? Will this child breathe? And Adam was a living creature.

In my youth, indeed until recently, I pretended not to believe in the resurrection of the dead. No way, thought I, arrogant in my knowledge. The culture nodded its approval. My Christianity was Stoic, which I disguised by calling it modern. It did not occur to me that I know as little about the dead as I do about the living. The culture told me there is nothing to be known, for the dead *are not*. This was the same culture that developed what Philip Slater has called the "toilet syndrome": when something is in the way, flush it down the pipe, after which it is supposed not to exist.

Depreciating the dead to zero value, we have cheapened life. Pretending that the dead have no future, we have deadened our own beginnings. For we all come from the dead. I do not mean only that our ancestors have rotted in their graves. I mean that our living selves are the animation of—what? Of something we must call either dead, as when we say "dead matter," or nothing.

How does anything get started? The question bothered Aristotle, who answered it with the philosophical myth of a "Prime Mover," an uncaused first cause, which the Scholastic theologians later identified with the Christian God. Paul Tillich's version of the question, more Platonic, was, "Why is there something and not nothing?" (Aristotelians like me prefer questions starting with *what* and *how*, while Platonists prefer to ask *why*.) Tillich answered his question with the philosophical symbol, "ground of Being," which he also identified with God.

Both these answers have ceased to work for me. I am too familiar with them. They come rushing in like some aunt or uncle dispensing home remedies I have long ago tried and outgrown. I find the question more interesting than any answer I have ever heard. How does anything get started? No, not even the question itself turns me on, but the situations in which the question arises. For example:

Two lovers lie abed. They have been living together for years. They are no longer drawn to each other by excitement of newness. They are even kept apart by memories of old misunderstandings. Their relation has by now a whole tangle of what R. D. Laing calls knots. They desire each other and yet they are inhibited, for fear of putting one more loop in the knots. At bedtime they retired, turned out the light; and the clock is ticking.

I imagine myself a film director. The script calls for the

scene to end with the couple making love. How does the love-making get started?

I lay by her side feeling resentment, loneliness, and desire all at once. More truly to say it, I wished for desire. I wanted her to break the ice. I wanted our love to be resurrected. Neither of us moved. Both wanting an initiative we were each terrified to make, we lay half paralyzed. In a manner of speaking, and this not entirely symbolic, we held our breath. There was more movement in the clock than in either of us. How does *anything* get started?

I have lived through that scene many times, and I still do not know the answer. There are, of course, many scripts. Sometimes no love-making starts. Sometimes we do it, and it's bad. Sometimes the kids crash in, or the phone rings. Sometimes we toss all night, or one of us does. Sometimes fatigue takes over and we sleep. Often we fight (how does *that* get started?) instead of fucking, and sometimes we do both. But occasionally we play the simpler and more miraculous script, the one all of us know and which would nevertheless be the hardest for the director and his actors to communicate: the paralysis is broken by some deliberate, tender, and definite act of love, an intentional creative move into the frightful void between us.

How does that initiative start? Where does it come from? When it comes from her, I am so grateful I do not ask. When it comes from me, I know that I do not know. Yet I know that *I* do it.

To know *why* I sometimes do and sometimes don't cross the threshold doesn't interest me. I leave that question to the theorists of psychodynamics. May God bless them. I am blessed with a question I love more: what begins a beginning? What am I to think of the phenomenon, happening all day long, of actions beginning from the heart of silence? What in the world *is* the impulse to movement?

And he breathed into him the breathing of life.

Friederich Schelling said, "the beginning of God has no beginning, for He is always beginning."

Since I am a religious person, it is only too easy for me to think, as the medieval theologians put it, that all beginnings are caused by God. On some days, this old answer of Aristotle and Aquinas is good enough; but on thinking days I don't like it, for it uses the name of God as a trump card to take the trick of logic and experience. The next trick is called responsibility, and the same trump takes that one, too. Pretty soon, all the tricks are in, and the divine-human bridge game has ended with a divine grand slam, then another and another through the whole set. Played piously, the divine-human game becomes a bore. If we start by saying God does everything, we must soon have a serpent in the garden. How does the *evil* impulse get started?

An action comprises two motives. The one we usually think about has to do with the end in view: my motive for going downstairs is to get the mail, or something like that. The other motive has to do with beginning, and it may have almost nothing to do with any end in sight. I stir, move, start for the sake of starting.

An Indian villager in Mexico told the visiting anthropologist the dancing would commence when the drum began to beat. "And when will that be?" asked the visitor, to which the Indian replied, "When it starts."

A prime motive gathers from chaos. Logically, there is nothing to say about it. In point of logic, no wiser nor clearer thing can be said about prime motive than the opening words of Genesis: "In the beginning." In point of logic, it makes no difference what subject and what verb come after that phrase. All stories begin "Once upon a time," followed by a subject and a verb.

Psychologically, a beginning may be experienced. When this happens, life becomes exciting, fascinating, fresh. I have an idea that most neuroses are symptoms of being cut off from the experience of beginning. Any therapy is effective to the extent that it restores that experience in the present. "Today is the first day of the rest of your life." . . . "Except a person be born again, he cannot enter the kingdom of heaven."

If I let the dead bury the dead, I may also let the dead find resurrection. Their doing so is not more mysterious than the appearance of any initiative in my life. I know as little of the start of my startings as I do of the time the dead may sleep. I have already been raised from the dead more than once. One time was that Sunday afternoon in 1925 when I first took in air. Even that was not the first time. One day I began to practice cell division. One day, months later *in utero*, I made my first muscular contraction. One day while sitting in church, I don't remember the year, it occurred to me that the grace of God the preacher babbled about was food I could eat. I ate. One day I realized I do not know where the literal stops and the metaphoric begins. In that moment the dead prosaic died and I was born, once more, into the holy fire.

When I grow dull, anxious, embittered, I return to my breathing. When I teach theology, the first thing I ask my students to do is notice their breathing. The taking of breath, analogue of every initiative in my life, is a point of coincidence in me between the divine and the human. Since we know nothing of how anything starts, it makes no difference whether we say I do it or God does it. The difference between God and the human lies not in origins, where all is equally mysterious and sacred, but in the qualities of actions once they *have* started. I recognize God as different from me not so much in the fact of beginnings as in the hope of endings. I wait upon God to accomplish what I know I cannot do, and for the sake of this waiting in hope I say that my beginnings and the beginnings of God are the same. My initiatives, which are really mine and not those of some puppet "caused" from outside, are at the same time the potential of God to will and to do the good work of liberation.

And he breathed into him the breathing of life, and Adam became a living creature.

Most of the time my breathing is involuntary. Yet at any moment I may become aware of it and bend it by voluntary control. My breath is me and not me, both statements true, equally true, equally life affirming. For I am, and am not, my conscious will. The minute I identify myself exclusively with my conscious will, I have taken the Satanic road to spiritual death. The minute I identify myself exclusively

with my preconscious being, I have taken the way of drift-
ing, which Shaw's Don Juan said was to be in hell.

To breathe knowingly is to become simultaneously
aware that life is a gift and that it is mine. When I sleep, I
continue to breathe. Every few seconds, with each inhalation, my life renews itself. This is a gift, mediated through
involuntary reflexes encoded in my genes during that long
adventure we call evolution. And when I awake, the same
involuntary motion continues while my mind is elsewhere.
I may not notice that I breathe until some shock or strenuous
effort or polluted atmosphere brings it to mind.

I have learned, however, to pay my breathing some
attention. I have learned to meditate on it for the sake of
experiencing my unity with all of life. This softens my
aggression. At times, though, I need my aggression, the
better to cope with conflict or danger. At such a moment, if
I have time, I deliberately modify my breathing. I make it
deeper, so as to feel it low in my belly (where the strong
emotions are) and high in my chest (where pride is felt) and
passing through my throat and mouth (instruments of
expression). This mustering of the breath abates anxiety
and alerts all my senses to observe the danger at hand. I become more rational even as my emotion becomes more free.

Between a quiet breathing that goes with meditation
and an active breathing in the presence of danger, I have
learned also a rhythmic breathing that goes with work,
music, and sex. From it comes pleasure far more gratifying
than my early and formal education ever led me to anticipate. Kneading dough at the bread board, dancing while the
beat is good, or moving into the motions of sex with my
partner, I come to a moment when the rhythm is secure and

I can go with it. Now there is no conflict between will and surrender. I am in a state my colleague Bob Neale calls "play," even if what I am doing is what other people call work. This rhythm is expressed in my breathing and cannot exist for me unless the breathing participates. I am at one with my activity, and through it I unite with all there is. For this, in my vocabulary, only the religious word *communion* will suffice. That is odd, for as a child (and long after) I used to hate Communion. It was long, tedious, pious. It seemed to be a matter of getting into some lofty frame of mind, some ethereal realm signified by the solemn organ and the silky wail of the choir. None of my experiences of honest participation in a rhythmic act was ever called communion, and so I had no sense of what it was all about. I don't think most of the preachers and congregations did, either. It was as if they were just doing, once a month, what they had been told to do.

When I get around to reorganizing the church, I shall ask it to look to its rhythm. The Black church often has plenty of it, which is why its services can be long without being boring. Some white churches have it, too, provided they have not lost the "old-time religion." But your mainline churches have become the victims of good taste, which is always atrocious because it means suppressing the rhythms of the body and dampening breath to a minimum. Therefore it is not surprising that most communion services have become like funerals. And not only that. They are like funerals for somebody over whom it is not even respectable to grieve!

When I think of the church, I hold my breath. The church I am looking for is a church that breathes. Either Jesus is, as the song says, the Lord of the Dance, or he is no Lord for me. Can the Lord of the Dance also be the prophet, priest, judge, king, savior, redeemer, Son of God, and all those other things he is said to be? I answer yes, but only if he is first the Lord of the Dance. Rhythm is the basic condition of life not at war with itself. From the time of the Gospel of John, Jesus has been identified with this basic condition by calling him the *logos*. The term is all but ruined now. *Logos* means structure. Jesus is said to be the *logos* or Word of God because he manifests the structure of God and creation. I add that the *logos moves*. It breathes. Has rhythm. Whatever doesn't is not the Word of God. Whatever lacks rhythm is bound unto death. That is why even pain, suffering, and evil are part of the Word of God, while a "heart of stone" is not. The Word of God may be crucified. What it may not do is sit like a bump on a log. It may not refuse to breathe, though it may willingly draw its final breath. The stories say that on his cross Jesus gave up the spirit. The word means breath. We will all one day give up our breath to whatever it was that summoned us to breathe on the first day. The question is whether, in the meantime, we have truly possessed our breathing and used it to conspire with the breathing of God.

And he breathed into him the breathing of life.

Do that to me, great breather of life. You did it already, I know. I know it best when I draw my own breath. When I know I am me and breathe my own breathing, I know you are you. Inhaling to the depth of my belly, I know that we conspire. The breath is mine and yours. We have not to decide whose turn is next. When I breathe, I breathe you.

Breathe in me, breath of God.